START YOUR BUSINESS

A Beginner's Guide

Third Edition

Compiled and Edited by
Vickie Reierson

The Oasis Press® / PSI Research
Central Point, Oregon

Published by The Oasis Press®/PSI Research
© 1993, 1995, 1998 by The Oasis Press®/PSI Research

This publication is designed to provide accurate and authoritative information
in regard to the subject matter covered. It is sold with the understanding that the
publisher is not engaged in rendering legal, accounting, or other professional
service. If legal advice or other expert assistance is required, the services of a
competent professional person should be sought.

> *— from a declaration of principles jointly adopted by a committee of
> the American Bar Association and a committee of publishers.*

Editor: Vickie Reierson
Compositors: Jan Olsson and C. C. Dickinson
Cover: Steven Burns based on design by Studio Silicon

Please direct any comments, questions, or suggestions regarding this book to
The Oasis Press®/ PSI Research:

Editorial Department
P.O. Box 3727
Central Point, OR 97502
(541) 479-9464
info@psi-research.com *email*

The Oasis Press® is a Registered Trademark of Publishing Services, Inc.,
an Oregon corporation doing business as PSI Research.

Start your business : a beginner's guide / compiled and edited by
  Vickie Reierson. — 3rd ed.
     p. cm. — (PSI successful business library)
  Includes index.
  ISBN 1-55571-485-4 (pbk.)
    1. New business enterprises—United States—Handbooks, manuals,
etc. I. Reierson, Vickie. II. Series.
HD62.5.S737 1998   98-48610
658.1'141--dc21

Printed in the United States of America
Third edition 10 9 8 7 6 5 4 3 2 1 0

 Printed on recycled paper when available.

Table of Contents

Preface

For more than twenty years, The Oasis Press® has been dedicated to providing accurate, timely, and practical business news and information to an ever-increasing number of entrepreneurs and self-employed professionals. Through the *PSI Successful Business Library*®, which boasts almost one hundred titles, and its *SmartStart Your* (State) *Business* series, written for nearly every state and the District of Columbia, The Oasis Press has carved out a unique niche as the "Leading Publisher of Small Business Information." Worldwide, The Oasis Press books line the shelves of countless business offices, retail stores, and business resource providers.

This third edition of *Start Your Business* is yet another example of The Oasis Press' continuing and unrelenting drive to meet the various needs of you, the budding or existing entrepreneur. Back in 1993, this book was created to help those wishing to start a business develop an organized and complete game plan before opening their doors. The Oasis Press recognized this need among start-up entrepreneurs — and noticed the lack of a worthy resource — and decided to take the ball and run with it.

Since that time, *Start Your Business* has been recognized as one of the "Top 40 Start-up Business Books" by *Inc.* magazine and is one of The Oasis Press' best-sellers. Its specific checklists and helpful resources have proven to be invaluable planning tools for those wanting to be organized and well-prepared before starting their new business.

But since the book's second edition in 1995, the face of small business has continued to change and evolve. New trends — such as increased competition, technology, home-based businesses, and the Internet — continue to influence how we approach starting a small business. That's why it was important to update *Start Your Business* to include some of these new trends and factors. You'll find some timely play-of-the-day moves in this third edition.

- New checklists on home-based office setup, small business lenders, and online marketing strategies.
- An entire new section on business management in Chapter 5 and text and new checklists on customer service, leadership skills, and profit-managing techniques.
- Each chapter's Helpful Resources section now includes new book titles that cover cutting-edge business topics and trends, as well as other handy business resources.
- New words of wisdom sprinkled throughout the Strategies and Tips sections.
- A fourth appendix featuring more than 50 business web sites to help streamline your research and information-gathering efforts.

This is all an effort here at The Oasis Press to keep you in-sync with what's happening in the small business world and help you be as on the ball as possible. This updated "rule book" for playing the business game should help ease any pre-game jitters and have you stepping up to the starting blocks in good shape!

Vickie Reierson
Editor

How to Use this Book

Start Your Business was created to help anyone who wants to start a business, but who doesn't quite know where to begin or what to do. Its general checklists and appendices are designed to jump-start this process and get you to organize and prioritize your thoughts and tasks in an easy, hopefully painless way!

While this may sound good to you, you still may be feeling slightly overwhelmed because of all the checkboxes and blank lines you see in the book.

How to Approach the Text

First of all, don't be intimidated! The eight topics discussed in this book may not all apply to your particular business. So before you get discouraged, simply look through the Table of Contents, or review the list below, and see which topics apply to your business concept or idea.

- Chapter 1 discusses the legal requirements that are necessary for starting a business. You can also get ideas and tips about where to locate your business and how to set up your office.
- Chapter 2 helps you decide whether you need sources of funding and where to look for funding. It also features handy checklists on business insurance and financial management issues.
- Chapter 3 highlights the importance of strategizing and planning your marketing activities before opening your doors.

From activities on how to conduct research to planning a media mix, you'll learn marketing basics at a glance.

- Chapter 4 informs you about all the activities and requirements that come into the picture once you hire an employee. This chapter emphasizes staffing procedures, government regulations for employers, and personnel paperwork.

- Chapter 5 is about production and management, and it provides information on overall issues regarding production, warehousing and shipping, and inventory, plus leadership and business management techniques.

- Chapter 6 deals with a hot topic: environmental concerns and laws. Find out what environmental laws apply to your business and what activities you'll need to complete. Learn about ways to save money and help the environment at the same time.

- Chapter 7 takes you through the process of developing a business plan. You may not have to do a business plan initially, but it's a good idea to think about doing one anyway. Business plans are a great way for you to investigate your business and be knowledgeable about its financial needs, marketing strategies, long-term goals, and operations.

- Chapter 8 concludes the book with a discussion on buying a business or franchise. This option may or may not apply to you; however, if you decide to buy a business or franchise, this chapter is a good reference and starting point.

So, if you're going to start your own service company out of your house and operate as a sole proprietorship, you'll not be concerned with Chapter 4 on employees or Chapter 8 on buying a business or franchise. You may not even be interested in doing a business plan (Chapter 7). The number of applicable topics you will have to deal with will vary depending on your particular situation.

Once you've determined which chapters you're interested in reviewing, first read through the chapters in their entirety. Don't stop to check off activities or make notes. Use your first read-through to familiarize yourself with the content and checklists, and to look up any unfamiliar terms in Appendix A. After your initial review is finished for each chapter, decide which chapter you need to concentrate on first, second, and so forth.

When you're ready to begin with your first chapter, be prepared to check off activities and write notes to yourself on the side.

You'll note the book occasionally provides you with blank lines for listing certain items. Feel free to jot down any notes on these lines.

As you read along, check off any activities that are required for your business and any activities that may prove helpful. You'll notice many of the activities listed throughout *Start Your Business* are not necessarily legal requirements, rather they're suggested options and precautions so you'll avoid making costly mistakes and be more prepared as a business owner.

Carefully evaluate each activity to see if it's something you feel you should do. If you have trouble understanding an activity, highlight it or mark it some way so you can come back to it later. Often, reading further in the text will help clarify these activities.

Helpful Resources

If you still have trouble understanding an activity or particular group of activities, refer to the Helpful Resources section, which is featured at the end of each chapter. This section provides you with additional resources for finding out more information regarding the topic area discussed in a chapter.

Remember, *Start Your Business* is a summary of several major business topics, and every detail cannot be covered. As a result, the Helpful Resources section was created to help you locate more information and materials.

Many of the resources listed in the Helpful Resources are Oasis Press and other publisher's business books, government agencies, and national associations. Some of the information in several of the chapters is drawn heavily from current Oasis Press books, which are good sources of information and readily available through bookstores. Nothing's more frustrating than to refer a person to a book or resource and find it's no longer in print, not published yet, or on back order. Consequently, all the resources listed in this edition, including all Oasis Press books, have been verified as available at the time of printing.

So, if you want to get more details on a particular subject, first look at the First Aid section, which immediately follows every chapter's introduction, to see which book is the best source for more information. Then, if you're interested in other aspects of the chapter's topics, check out the Helpful Resources section.

Plan of Action Worksheets

Once you've finished reviewing all the checklists in a chapter, and you've marked off those activities you want to do, you're ready for the Plan of Action worksheets located at the end of every chapter. These worksheets are designed as an organizing and tracking tool for the checked-off activities in the chapter.

How to use the worksheets is mainly up to you. The basic premise of the worksheets is to provide a convenient place for you to organize, prioritize, and track the necessary activities. The worksheets provide columns for you to indicate what action needs to be taken, when it should be started, who'll be responsible for carrying it out, and what the deadline is for each activity.

If you feel there are too many checked-off activities in the chapter to list all at once on the worksheets, start off with just a few of the activities that seem most pertinent and time-consuming. Pick the top 25, for example, and list them in the order of priority you feel they should be completed. When you have prioritized and organized these activities, you can pick the next 25 and go from there.

Another strategy may be to list all the activities you've marked off in the chapter under the "Action to be Taken" column on the worksheets. Then, using highlighters, go back and highlight (in a particular color) all the activities that need to be done first. Pick another highlighter color for all the activities you want to do next, and so on. Once you're done prioritizing, you can go back and determine who will do what, and when.

Regardless of the method you'll employ for organizing and tracking your activities, be sure to cut out each Plan of Action worksheet so you can make several copies. You most likely will need several copies for each chapter.

When you've done the Plan of Action worksheets for each of the appropriate chapters, you'll have a good handle on what it'll take to start your business. These Plan of Action worksheets will prove quite valuable in getting you into the business game in tip top shape. You'll have a game plan and sense of what it's going to take to win!

Appendices

This edition of *Start Your Business* features four appendices:

- Appendix A provides many business term definitions that will hopefully clarify some of the activities in the chapters, plus prove to be educational for some.

- Appendix B is a current listing of all the state director offices for the Small Business Development Center (SBDC) network. SBDCs are valuable sources of free information and advice for small business owners. The state director's office can refer you to the SBDC nearest you. If you're starting a business, this office is a great resource.

- Appendix C lists national and state-specific business publications that may prove helpful in your research regarding new business and industry trends, marketing, and business plans. They may also prove helpful in keeping you on top of national and state legislation that may affect your business.

- Appendix D is a compilation of some of the savviest business web sites online today. Take full advantage of these free, info-packed resources as you prepare and train for the business game. You'll find all sorts of info and tips that'll make opening (and running) your business much easier.

Lightbulb Information

You may have noticed a lightbulb icon sprinkled throughout this book. This icon signals there are some additional thoughts and questions to the activity statement that immediately precedes it.

 The lightbulb information is provided to prompt you to think about related items or issues that may help you accomplish or complete an activity easier and more fully. Hopefully, this information will help you cover more of the business game basics and avoid costly mistakes.

Sometimes, the lightbulb information provides how-to instructions or most likely, it'll be stated in a question format to encourage your thinking process and creativity.

The Bottom Line

By reading and working your way through *Start Your Business*, you're going to learn several different aspects of starting a business. From the smallest of details involving business filings and taxes to the larger areas dealing with research and long-term planning, you'll come out ahead because of this book's checklists and tips. You'll probably learn about requirements you never knew existed, review areas you were familiar with but may have forgotten, and realize various tasks you can do to help you be a better business owner.

In short, *Start Your Business* will guide you to a better opening day and a more informed beginning. Let the business game begin!

Chapter 1

Getting Off on the Right Foot —
Start-Up Issues

Introduction

Entrepreneurs! On your mark, set, GO!

While it's easy to get caught up in the excitement of starting your own business, playing the business game is like playing any other strenuous sport — you need to be in good shape and well-prepared. And that's exactly what this book and initial chapter is all about. It's a time-out for you eager entrepreneurs to sit down and plan out your strategies and learn some of the basic rules of biz ownership.

Depending on your situation, you may have already decided on some of the basic start-up considerations outlined in this chapter. If you've already dealt with some of these issues, this chapter will be a good review of your initial impressions and decisions regarding what it takes to start your own business. If you've not made some of these basic start-up decisions, then this will be a good starting point.

Some of the fundamental questions you may have already answered by now (or which you should answer after reading this chapter) are:

- Will your business be a sole proprietorship, a partnership, a corporation, or a limited liability company (LLC)? Refer to the Glossary for definitions of each form.
- Where will you locate your office or place of business?
- How will your office be set up? What equipment will you buy initially?

These questions, of course, are only a few of the many you'll need to answer before starting your business. Other issues, such as start-up financing, how to write your business plan, and how to develop a marketing strategy, are detailed in later chapters. For now, however, the issues and considerations raised here will help you get off on the right foot.

First Aid for Start-Up Issues

 When it comes to getting an all-in-one guide for starting a biz, there's no better resource than the series, *SmartStart Your* (State) *Business*, which is dedicated to providing a how-to business book for every state, plus the District of Columbia. Each book discusses everything a new entrepreneurial player needs to know — from your business' legal form, name, and licenses to obtaining financing, customers, and employees. It's a hefty book for helping you build your business muscles and getting off to a strong start.

State-specific and federal government rules and red tape won't seem as daunting with this savvy, start-up resource. And its beefy appendices outline all the forms you'll need to get started, as well as a multitude of agency and business resources you can call for more information. To get your state's copy of *SmartStart*, contact your local bookstore, or:

The Oasis Press
(800) 228-2275

And if you're at the stage where you're still trying to decide which business is right for you, look no further! The Oasis Press book, *Which Business? Help in Selecting Your New Venture*, can save the day with its real-life insights into scores of different business opportunities.

General Requirements for All New Start-Ups

Regardless of whether your business is a sole proprietorship, a partnership, a corporation, or a limited liability company (LLC), you'll be required to make certain filings and registrations with government agencies, pay certain taxes, and complete certain research before opening your doors.

The first checklist in this section highlights some general start-up considerations to act on as soon as possible, regardless of your business' legal form. This checklist focuses on nongovernmental considerations, whereas the subsequent checklists deal with general government requirements on the federal, state, and local levels.

Additional requirements that apply specifically to sole proprietorships, partnerships, or corporations are outlined in the next section of this chapter, and additional requirements for any business that will hire employees are covered in Chapter 4.

The main goal of this section is to highlight the initial requirements for any business starting up in any state. Review these checklists carefully so you learn the business game basics.

General Start-Up Considerations Checklist

No matter what type of business you'll start or what form of legal organization you choose, you'll need to think about some general start-up considerations. The activities listed below will provide an initial plan of action.

- [ ] Determine your legal form of business organization. (See your *SmartStart* state book for the pros and cons of each.)
    - [ ] Sole proprietorship
    - [ ] General or limited partnership
    - [ ] Corporation
    - [ ] Limited liability company (LLC)

- [ ] Learn what it means to elect S corporation status and see if it's a benefit for your business.

- [ ] List all the possible names for your business. Avoid descriptive names, initials, family surnames, geographic names, and names identical to or very similar to ones already in use.

_____

_____

_____

_____

_____

_____

_____

☐ Rank the top ten names you have listed above, and research them to see which ones are available for use.

☐ Choose the name of your business.

☐ Create a logo for your business, if desired.

☐ Choose the name of your product or service.

☐ Consider the types of insurance you'll need to obtain before opening your doors. Chapter 2 coaches you on business insurance.

☐ Determine the steps you'll take to lessen your personal liability regarding the business.

> Will you incorporate to avoid personal liability?
>
> Will you purchase a personal liability policy?
>
> Will you create clear, written company policies to verify your procedures? See Chapter 4 for more on company policies.

☐ Look for reputable accountants and attorneys to work with you.

> Do they have satisfied clients who will give recommendations?
>
> Do they have an expertise in business law?
>
> How are their fees compared to others in the local area?

☐ Do a complete financial overview of your start-up venture. Chapter 2 specifies how to do this. Consider:

> How much money will you need for the first six months of operations?
>
> What are your initial start-up expenses?
>
> Where will you get additional sources of funds when necessary?

☐ Determine if your business will need employees. See Chapter 4.

☐ Write a business plan. Refer to Chapter 7.

☐ Organize your initial marketing strategies. Refer to Chapter 3.

☐ Research your state for a one-stop business assistance center.

Federal General Requirements Checklist

This checklist covers all the general requirements when dealing with the federal government as a new business owner, regardless of your business' legal form. Review the checklist carefully to determine what actions you'll need to take on behalf of your business. Agencies you need to contact for more information are often listed in parentheses after the activity.

☐ Do a federal trade name, trademark, or service mark search. (Patent and Trademark Office in Washington, D.C.)

☐ Determine if you need a federal license to operate your business.

> Most new small businesses do not require federal licensing. Some of the businesses that do require federal licensing include investment firms, broadcast stations, common carrier companies, firearm dealers, meat packagers, and drug producers.

☐ Obtain information on how and when to make quarterly federal estimated income tax payments. (IRS)

☐ Learn about your obligations for reporting certain federal tax information on the 1099 form series. (IRS)

☐ Review the environmental regulations set forth in the Comprehensive Environmental Response, Compensation and Liability Act (CERCLA or also known as Superfund) and the Resource Conservation and Recovery Act (RCRA). (U.S. Department of Environmental Quality)

State and Local General Requirements Checklist

In addition to the federal requirements, it's equally important you take care of state and local general requirements. In general, most states have similar registration requirements and taxes; however, each state's unique so researching both state and local requirements through your various state and local agencies or one-stop business centers is a good game plan.

This way, you won't miss any registration or tax not mentioned in this checklist.

☐ Do a state and local trade name search to determine if the name you've chosen for your business, product, or service is identical or confusingly similar to a name that's already in use. To do this:

    ☐ Contact your secretary of state's office and your local county clerk's office to request this information.

    ☐ Look through local phone directories, business directories, and publications for any similar name.

☐ Obtain a local business license from your city hall or county office.

☐ Obtain a state business license, plus any additional licenses that may be required for your particular profession or occupation, from the appropriate state licensing agency.

☐ If your state has an income tax, know how to report your earnings or losses on the appropriate returns.

☐ Determine how to make state estimated income tax filings, if applicable.

☐ Register your business with the appropriate state revenue or tax department for any required seller's permit or sales tax license, whichever is applicable.

Is a separate permit required for each place of business?

Where do you need to display the permit(s)?

Are you required to display it on the opening day of business?

☐ Investigate your obligation as a seller for collecting and remitting any sales and use tax in your state.

☐ Determine how to register your fictitious business name with both the state and local governments.

How does your state define a fictitious business name?

What application forms will you have to complete?

Are there any fees required?

☐ Contact your state and local tax departments to inquire about any and all taxes you will need to be aware of as a business. Ask about:

☐ Excise taxes on such items as tobacco, fuels, and hazardous substances, if applicable to your particular type of business;

☐ Inventory and equipment taxes;

☐ Motor vehicle registration fees; and

☐ Property taxes.

☐ Research any state or local environmental laws that may apply to your type of business, such as air quality and hazardous waste disposal requirements.

Specific Requirements for Various Legal Forms of Business

Each legal form of doing business has its own advantages and disadvantages, and which one you choose for your new business is a decision only you can make. The four main forms of doing business are:

- Sole proprietorships
- Partnerships
- Corporations
- Limited liability companies (LLCs)

Refer to the Glossary for definitions of these four legal forms of doing business. Once you know which legal form of business you'll use, review the appropriate checklist in this section to find out the requirements that are specific to your legal form. Remember you need to do all of the activities listed in the previous section, General Requirements for All New Start-Ups, regardless of your legal form.

Sole Proprietorship Checklist

Because sole proprietors have relatively few requirements for starting a business, this checklist is shorter than the others in this section.

☐ File *Form SS-4, Application for Employer Identification Number (EIN),* with the IRS, even if you won't hire any employees.

☐ Prepare to include *Schedule C* with your federal individual income tax return, *Form 1040.* You're required to report all your income or loss from the business on this return.

☐ If your state has a personal income tax (or an equivalent tax), then research how to report any income or loss from your business on your state tax returns by contacting your state tax department or your accountant.

☐ Research the federal self-employment tax by contacting the IRS.

> The self-employment tax is a Social Security and Medicare tax for those who work for themselves. You're required to pay this tax as a sole proprietor, as well as file *Schedule SE* with your *Form 1040* tax return.

☐ Double-check with your secretary of state's office (or its equivalent) to see if there are any additional state registration requirements or filings that weren't included in the State and Local General Requirements Checklist.

Partnership Checklist

The checklist includes requirements for both general and limited partnerships. Those requirements pertaining to limited partnerships are indicated by an (LP only) at the end of the requirement. The requirements without the (LP only) following them apply to both general and limited partnerships.

☐ Though not an official requirement by any governmental agency, consider writing a partnership agreement for your partnership.

    ☐ Have this agreement signed by each partner.

    ☐ Have your attorney and accountant review the agreement.

☐ Investigate federal reporting procedures regarding partnership income by contacting the IRS and requesting information on how to:

    ☐ File federal *Form 1065*, a partnership information return; and

    ☐ Report your share of partnership income or loss on your federal income tax return.

☐ If your state has a personal income tax (or an equivalent tax), then research how to report any income or loss from your partnership on your state tax returns by contacting your state tax department or your accountant.

☐ Research the federal self-employment tax by contacting the IRS. The self-employment tax is a Social Security and Medicare tax for those who work for themselves. You're required to pay it as a partner.

☐ Even if your partnership will not have employees, you're still required to file *Form SS-4, Application for Employer Identification Number (EIN)*, with the IRS. This filing will register you with the IRS and provide you with the EIN that you'll use for tax filing purposes.

☐ File a certificate of limited partnership with your secretary of state's office and see if you're required to file copies of this certificate with the counties in which you plan to do business. (LP only)

    ☐ Check to see if a fee is charged for this filing. (LP only)

☐ Double-check with the secretary of state's office to see if there are any additional state registration requirements for general or limited partnerships that weren't included in the State and Local General Requirements Checklist.

Corporation Checklist

When you decide to incorporate, you take on a number of additional start-up requirements. Because incorporating is often confusing and complex, it's a good idea to consult an attorney and get educated on corporation ins and outs. Two Oasis Press books, *InstaCorp: Incorporate in Any State* and *The Essential Corporation Handbook*, are good starting points. The checklist below gives you a hint of all the topics these books cover.

☐ Choose which type of corporation you wish to operate.

    ☐ Close corporation

    ☐ Foreign corporation

    ☐ General business corporation or C corporation

    ☐ Nonprofit corporation

    ☐ Professional corporation

☐ Choose a state of incorporation.

☐ Get a corporate address.

☐ Select a corporate name.

    ☐ Have your corporate name include the words, "corporation," "incorporated," "company," "limited," or "association."

☐ File your corporation's articles of incorporation with your secretary of state's office.

☐ Check with the appropriate state agency — usually the secretary of state's office — to see what fees are required for incorporation.

☐ Adopt a set of bylaws.

☐ Designate a registered office or registered agent who can and will be available for the service and process of official correspondence from the courts or state governments to your corporation.

☐ Decide if your corporation will issue stock.

    What kinds of stock are there and which ones do you want to offer?

    How will your corporation pay out dividends?

    How will your shareholders' agreement be drawn up?

    Which securities laws will you need to comply with?

☐ Elect a board of directors and schedule when it will meet.

    ☐ Ensure someone will be responsible for taking minutes of the meeting and distributing them accordingly.

☐ Keep detailed corporate records once your corporation has begun to operate. This will include records such as:

    ☐ The minutes from all board of director and shareholder meetings;

- [ ] A record of all actions taken by the board of directors or shareholders without a meeting;
- [ ] All written communication by the corporation to the shareholders;
- [ ] A list of the names and addresses of current officers and directors; and
- [ ] The most recent annual report of the corporation that was submitted to the secretary of state.

- [ ] If you'll do business outside your state of incorporation, obtain a certificate of authority from each state where you plan to do business. A certificate of authority can be obtained through the secretary of state's office in each state where you plan to do business.
  - [ ] Pay any appropriate fees for these filings.
  - [ ] Include a certificate of good standing with your filing information. This certificate is available through the secretary of state's office in the state where you incorporate.

- [ ] Contact the IRS to receive instructions on how to report corporate income tax on *Form 1120*.

- [ ] Obtain plenty of federal tax deposit coupons from the IRS so your corporation can make its estimated income tax payments easily.

- [ ] File *Form SS-4, Application for Employer Identification Number,* with the IRS to receive your employer identification number. You must do this filing even if you don't have employees.

- [ ] Contact the state tax department to receive instructions on how to pay its corporate income or franchise tax.

Will you have to pay estimated payments for any state income tax? What is the minimum amount for any franchise tax in your state?

- [ ] Request that the state tax department send you information on all the corporate tax requirements within the state. This will ensure you don't forget anything regarding the state's tax requirements for corporations.

- [ ] Register with your state's secretary of state, tax authority, and other agencies to receive a business account number.

- [ ] Make a note that your corporation must file annual reports once it's up and running.

- [ ] Comply with both state and federal securities laws.

Limited Liability Company Checklist

Requirements for LLC organization vary from state to state; however, this checklist provides some basic overall LLC requirements. To find out more regarding this form of doing business, get a copy of *The Essential Limited Liability Company Handbook* from The Oasis Press.

☐ File articles of organization with your secretary of state's office.

☐ Because nearly all states require an LLC to have at least two owners, consider who'll be your co-owner.

☐ Check with the appropriate state agency — usually the secretary of state's office — to see what fees and registration are required for an LLC.

☐ If your state has an income tax (or an equivalent tax), then research how to report any income or loss of your LLC on your state and federal tax returns by contacting your local tax or revenue department.

☐ Double-check with the secretary of state's office to see if there are any additional state registration requirements for limited liability companies that weren't included in the State and Local General Requirements Checklist.

Location! Location! Location!

Deciding where to locate your business can often mean the difference between winning the business game and losing it. You may have the highest-quality product or the most helpful service in your area, but if you don't locate your business appropriately, you can lose a lot of money through missed foot traffic opportunities or an insufficient pool of qualified labor.

The reasons to locate in a certain place vary depending on your type of business. For example, if you're going to open a restaurant or retail business, you're obviously going to want to ideally locate in an area where there is a lot of available parking, a good flow of walk-in and drive-by traffic, and little competition.

If you're a manufacturer or wholesaler, you'll be more interested in a site that's close to major transportation services, has a large pool of skilled labor available, and has sufficient access to water, sewer, and other vital services.

Even though the checklists below cover several general aspects of locating a retail or nonretail business, don't skimp on this start-up consideration. Do your homework. Get some solid advice and info on how to choose a location for your new biz from various sources, including your local chamber of commerce, real estate agents, planning department, or economic development organization. You can also get a how-to book, such as *Location, Location, Location: How to Select the Best Site for Your Business*, for more on the site selection process. Use these checklists as a guide for getting started on your location research.

General Location Considerations Checklist

This checklist is a potpourri of tips and activities you can consider when deciding where to locate your new business in a particular place. Most of these considerations apply to all types of businesses, with the possible exception of home-based businesses.

☐ Consider the advantages of leasing your place of business, such as less financial risk and the option of subletting, or avoiding a long-term rental commitment. If you do decide to lease your business' location, consider including the following items in any agreement you sign:

    ☐ The length of the lease;

    ☐ The amount of rent, how it's determined, and when it's payable;

    ☐ The description of the space to be occupied;

    ☐ The option to renew;

    ☐ Any restrictions on remodeling or other modifications to the interior of the space and who owns any leasehold improvements;

    ☐ Any restrictions on the posting of signs on the outside of the building or in the surrounding yard;

    ☐ Protection from co-occupancy or nearby occupancy by competing businesses;

    ☐ The option to purchase the space;

    ☐ Landlord responsibilities regarding improvements for fire, health, and safety issues;

    ☐ Insurance requirements for the landlord and tenant;

    ☐ Reconstruction timing and requirements in case of fire, earthquake, or other natural disasters;

    ☐ Status of tenant, if the space is sold; and

    ☐ The possibility of subletting by the tenant.

☐ Always have your attorney review any real estate or lease agreements.

☐ Research any environmental restrictions that may apply to your business if it locates in a particular area.

☐ Check on local zoning ordinances, regulations, and other land use restrictions before selecting a site for your new business.

> What signs, if any, can you erect? Is there a size restriction?
>
> Is your proposed business site zoned for commercial use?
>
> What about off-street parking? Will this be a problem?
>
> Will you be able to get city services, such as water and sewer?
>
> Will you need any permits for remodeling or constructing your business?

☐ Determine the kind of security system you'll need to install by investigating the crime rate in your location and talking to law enforcement officials.

☐ Determine the cost of purchasing the real estate as opposed to leasing it.

> How do the costs compare for the short and long term?
>
> Are there any advantages to doing one over the other?

☐ Be sure to investigate only the sites most appropriate for your type of business. For instance, as a manufacturer, don't waste a lot of time looking at prime downtown retail locations; concentrate on industrial parks or other such avenues.

☐ See if any local economic development agency is available to help you find a suitable site.

☐ Contact the local governments — for example, the city hall or county clerk's office — to determine what, if any, taxes or permits will apply to your business within a particular area.

☐ Find a real estate agent to help you look for a possible site for your business.

☐ Find out what energy sources are available at each site and whether they are adequate for your type of machinery, equipment, or production process.

> Are the energy costs within your budget?
>
> Can you get alternative energy sources, if you so desire?
>
> What's involved in setting up a business account with the public utilities available in your area?
>
> What's the usual waiting period for receiving utility services?

☐ Evaluate each site as it is now, and then try to forecast how it will be situated within the short- and long-term future.

> Is there a possibility of residential development nearby?
>
> What are the population trends for the area? Are they increasing or decreasing?
>
> What is the water source like? Is it dependable?
>
> Can you expand or reduce your space easily?
>
> Do you anticipate commercial growth in that area?
>
> Is there additional space or property you could purchase in the future?

Retail Location Considerations Checklist

If you're going to be operating a retail store, then this checklist — and the Oasis Press book, *Retail in Detail: How to Start and Manage a Small Retail Business* — is for you. Review the considerations outlined below from this book before deciding where to locate your retail business.

☐ Research the population trends for the local county or city to see if your particular business will have enough support, in terms of a potential market, to survive.

☐ Determine the number of competitors already established in the area and whether or not any more plan to locate there.

☐ Study the reaction of the local community to businesses similar to yours.

> Was the response favorable, or did the community tend to stay with the more established business?
>
> Is your type of business considered "undesirable" to the local neighborhood or community? If so, consider another area.

☐ Evaluate how accessible the site is for walk-in or drive-by traffic.

> Is there plenty of parking around your location?
>
> Are mass transit stops nearby?
>
> Are all the popular shops on your side of the street? Or will people have to cross the street to come to your door?

☐ Find out how close you are to major boulevards, highways, shopping centers, and civic centers to make sure your business location is more visible.

☐ Determine if the site's atmosphere and physical surroundings attract your target market.

- ☐ Make sure the zoning restrictions in your location allow your type of business.

- ☐ Research the foot traffic and the automobile traffic that is going by your potential site.

    > Are the numbers good enough to warrant consideration?
    >
    > How is your target market reflected in those numbers?

- ☐ Ensure you'll have enough space for your needs.

- ☐ Determine how close you are to fire and police departments and what kind of protection is available.

- ☐ Research the costs of the different types of spaces available and carefully review the rules of the lessor.

- ☐ Make sure the space has or will have nice restrooms and other appropriate employee/customer facilities.

- ☐ Determine how the location and facilities enhance your business' image.

Nonretail Location Considerations Checklist

If you'll be operating a nonretail business, then your considerations will focus more on the physical and logistical aspects and less on customer accessibility and visibility. If you're going to be operating a nonretail business from home, then you'll also want to ensure the zoning laws in your neighborhood allow your type of business and that you'll be able to erect signs and remodel to suit your needs.

- ☐ Ensure that the physical aspects of the site are what you need.

    > Is there room to expand if necessary?
    >
    > Are there any bogholes, swamps, or other similar problems with the ground surface?
    >
    > Are there any awkward slopes, rocky spots, or timber to be removed?

- ☐ See if the location is conveniently situated in a geographic area that is easy to get to and not too far out of the way for both you and any employees you will hire.

- ☐ Research the availability of skilled labor in the area.

    > Will there be an adequate supply of the types of skilled workers you will need for your type of business?

☐ Determine if any building you evaluate or build has:

    ☐ Employee restrooms, break areas, or designated smoking areas;

    ☐ Enough space for start-up operations, plus room to grow;

    ☐ Enough electrical outlets and power capability for your company's needs, such as for computers, production equipment, and heating and air conditioning;

    ☐ Complied with all accessibility requirements under the Americans with Disabilities Act (ADA);

    ☐ An adequate shipping and receiving area that can accommodate the type of transportation services you'll be using;

    ☐ Plenty of phone jacks and lines to handle all your business calls; and

    ☐ Sound structural design.

☐ See who your neighbors will be and if they're competitors or compatible businesses.

☐ Find the suppliers you'll need for your business and see if the location is convenient for them.

☐ Ensure the availability of raw materials, adequate sanitation, and utilities.

☐ See how convenient the location is for any transportation services you will use for your business.

    Is it out of the way for delivery and pickup trucks?

    Are you near an airport, railroad station, or water port? Which ones are the most important for you to be near?

☐ Determine what support services you'll need to run your business and see if your business location is convenient for all concerned. For instance:

    Where is your office supplier located?

    Where are necessary repair services located?

Office Set Up

Once you've decided on a location for your new business, it's time to think about how you'll set up your office. And depending on which type of business you open, this may be an easy or not-so-easy job. But the bottomline is you'll want it to be functional, organized, and comfortable.

When first starting your business, try to buy only those supplies necessary for start-up. You'll want to spend wisely at this point and you can always buy more supplies as your needs and budget warrant. Be prepared financially for your initial start-up office costs, and include these expenses in your budgeting process.

If you take the time now to consider what you'll need in your office on opening day, you'll jumpstart your chances of being efficient and on top of all the paperwork and recordkeeping that goes with being your own boss. The checklists below are designed to help you consider all the office details before opening day, whether you're in a retail biz or not. And since so many of you entrepreneurs are home-based, we've included a brief checklist for you to consider as well.

Office Set Up Checklist

Begin to formulate an idea of how you'd like to have your office organized. Remember this is a general checklist and your type of business may warrant some special equipment, furniture, or supplies not listed.

☐ List all your anticipated office furniture needs for initial start-up, for example, desks, chairs, file cabinets, and lamps.

Will you need to include interior decorating items, such as plants, rugs, and window coverings?

Will it be more advantageous for you to rent or own your office furniture?

What about the possibility of buying used or new furniture?

☐ List all your anticipated office equipment needs for initial start-up, for example, personal computers, fax machines, telephones, typewriters, printers, and copiers. List how many of each you'll need.

_____

_____

_____

_____

_____

_____

_____

_____

☐ Have your business stationery and company logo designed and printed. Other business paperwork you may need to have printed include:

☐ Business cards   ☐ Purchase orders

☐ Business envelopes   ☐ Receipts

☐ Company checks   ☐ Sales orders

☐ Invoices   ☐ Shipping labels

> How much will it cost for the design of a logo and to print your letterhead, invoices, and business cards?
>
> How will you design your company's in-house invoices and purchase orders?

☐ Estimate your office supply needs — such as paper, pens, tape, phone message pads, paper clips, Post-it Notes, calendars, dictionaries, hanging file folders, and staplers — and shop around for the best prices. Include:

☐ Computer supplies and needs, such as computer paper, disks, disk labels, software programs, accessories, toner, and technical support services.

☐ Create a process and get a box for handling petty cash.

☐ Set up and organize your filing system for the office.

☐ Jot down whatever office supplies you will need for this system.

_____

_____

_____

_____

_____

☐ Establish a basic form of bookkeeping for your front desk needs.

☐ Obtain a ledger.

☐ Have a cash receipts journal.

☐ Set up a process for handling mail.

> Get a "waste" basket, an "interesting" mail basket, and an "action" mail basket, and touch your mail only once as it goes into one of these three boxes.

☐ Contact your local post office and get general information on how to:

    ☐ Determine postage amounts for different parcels and letters;

    ☐ Organize a bulk mailing; and

    ☐ Use business reply cards.

> Will you use a postage meter or purchase stamps?
>
> What is your monthly estimate for postage expenses?

☐ Choose a delivery service, such as Federal Express or United Parcel Service, and learn about its schedules, fees, and services.

☐ Establish your regular business office hours.

☐ Determine how you or your receptionist will answer the phone.

> What greeting will you use?
>
> How will phone transfers be made? Will you transfer directly to each person, or will you screen calls so the person being called knows the name of the person calling?
>
> What kind of holding messages or music will you employ, if any?

☐ Decide if you will use a telephone answering service or machine to answer business calls that come in after hours. Also consider:

> How many lines will you need?
>
> Will you have a fax machine?
>
> Will you have voice mail?
>
> What about a toll-free, 800 number?

☐ Investigate the cost and procedure for getting a telephone number for your business and listing that number in the local phone directory.

☐ Decide which phone services your business will need (and budget for them).

> Should you have calling waiting, forwarding, or voice mail?
>
> Will you need conference calling or data and voice differentiation?
>
> What about video conferencing?

☐ Set up business letter models for common correspondence applicable to your type of business.

☐ Research where to find the best buys on office furniture and supplies.

Home-Based Office Checklist

Home is where the heart is, but these days, home's also where the biz is too! And when you bring your business into your home, you often have some additional and trickier decisions to make when it comes to office set up — like which room do you get and can you lock the kids out? The book, *Moonlighting: Earn a Second Income at Home*, by Jo Frohbieter-Mueller is a terrific start-up guide for any of you do-it-at-homers.

☐ Decide on a location for the home office. Consider:

    ☐ Accessibility for yourself and customers.

    ☐ Proximity to the television, kids, and fridge.

    ☐ Office atmosphere, like lighting, temperature, and space.

    ☐ The type of work you'll be doing.

☐ Ask your accountant about the office-in-the-home deduction tax advantages and disadvantages.

☐ Set guidelines for any children or other relatives who might share the house with your biz.

    What will your office hours be?

    Will customers be coming to and from the office?

    Which phone or phone lines should family members answer or not?

☐ Consider buying well-designed office furniture to avoid back pain, carpel tunnel syndrome, and other related office ailments.

☐ Get the room outfitted with electrical outlets and light fixtures to accommodate your office equipment.

☐ Evaluate your neighborhood's zoning laws to ensure there's no conflict regarding your business and its operations.

☐ Get phone lines to your home office.

☐ Consider ways to make your home office professional-looking.

☐ Research home business risks and any necessary insurance coverage.

Strategies and Tips

 Starting your own business takes inspiration, drive, and hard work. You can succeed, but you'll have to work at it. Some of the business basics discussed in this and the following chapters will hopefully lessen your initial concern of covering all the bases before you open your doors. Read the additional strategies and tips below for encouragement and reference. Be sure to complete the Plan of Action for Start-Up Issues worksheet to help organize your start-up thoughts, concerns, and activities.

- Create a dynamic duo and partner up with someone who really excels in an important area of business that's your weak point. Good partners can tip the scales towards success.

- Being your own boss provides a sense of pride and freedom, but remember, the hours, responsibilities, and lower-than-expected financial rewards may take an initial toll. Go into business with your rose-colored glasses on the counter.

- Educate yourself as much as possible about operating and running a small business. Attend seminars, college classes, and workshops. Connect up with a mentor. Take advantage of the Internet and visit small business web sites with chat rooms. Get as much first-hand feedback on what it takes to succeed in business as possible.

- If feasible, name your product or service the same as your business. This double exposure really helps your name recognition and visibility.

- Dress, act, and speak in a professional manner and conduct an organized, smooth-running office. It does wonders for your credibility and attracts quality customers.

- Go to your state's business or economic department for a start-up business packet. These offices have tons of free, practical resources for starting a biz.

Helpful Resources

Here are some savvy start-up resources to consider. For more of the same, you can refer to the appendices in the back of the book for info on SBDCs, biz magazines and other publications, and online resources for small business.

American Home Business Association
(800) 664-2422

Dedicated to helping the work-at-home biz owners.

Legal Guide for Starting and Running a Small Business
Nolo Press
(800) 992-6656

This book emphasizes avoiding legal problems on leases in particular. Make sure the landlord doesn't give you the short end of the stick.

Naming Your Business and Its Products and Services
The P. Gaines Publishing Company
(800) 578-3853

A fun-to-read book on how to name your business.

National Association for the Self-Employed (NASE)
(800) 232-NASE

If you take the plunge into self-employment, join this association. NASE is committed to helping you meet the challenges of making your biz a success. More than 300,000 members strong, it gives you a strong voice in the nation's capitol.

National Association of Women Business Owners (NAWBO)
(301) 608-2590
(800) 55-NAWBO

The NAWBO strengthens the voice of all women business owners. Membership provides access to valuable networking and assistance on the local chapter level; special discounts on goods and services; and public representation at all levels of government.

National Business Association (NBA)
(800) 456-0440

A nonprofit organization dedicated to assisting small biz owners in achieving their goals. It offers an array of benefits and services that provide monetary discounts and other quality resources.

National Federation of Independent Business (NFIB)
Attn: Membership Services
(800) NFIB NOW

Join forces with the largest small business organization and most effective advocate. Going strong since 1943, these guys do what it takes to preserve free enterprise around the country.

Records Management
American Management Association (AMA)
1 (888) 281-5092

This book provides guidance on how to perfect the art of recordkeeping, from starting up a program to maintaining a records center, designing filing systems, and handling forms and reports.

SBA Answer Desk
U.S. Small Business Administration
(800) 827-5722

The SBA Answer Desk is a series of prerecorded messages that helps answer many questions new start-ups may have about financing or starting a business. You can also request a listing of SBA publications from the SBA Answer Desk.

Small Business Advancement National Center
(501) 450-5300

This center collects and disseminates demographic and statistical information on Small Business Institutes (SBIs), which are located on college campuses throughout the United States. They offer free business assistance, free, confidential consulting, and recommendations to various business problems. Contact a university near you to see if it has an SBI, or contact the above number.

Small Business Service Bureau, Inc. (SBSB)
(800) 222-5678

The SBSB is a national small business organization that provides small business owners with money-saving group benefits and services and legislative advocacy in all the states and Washington, D.C.

Small-Time Operator: How to Start Your Own Business, Keep Your Books, Pay Your Taxes, & Stay Out of Trouble
Bell Springs Publishing
(800) 515-8050

Overall general start-up book that tackles the technical aspects of starting a business. Revised annually.

Wage Slave No More: The Independent Contractor's Legal Guide
Nolo Press
(800) 992-6656

Everything you need to know if you're going be self-employed.

Working Solo: The Real Guide to Freedom & Financial Success with Your Own Business
John Wiley
(800) 222-7656

Everything you need to be an efficient and successful one-person biz — tips and good advice from a biz expert.

Working Solo Sourcebook
John Wiley
(800) 222-7656

A handy, easy-to-use reference book to more than 1,200 essential business resources — each ready to guide you on the path to business success.

Helpful Resources from The Oasis Press

The Oasis Press — The Leading Publisher of Small Business Information also has a collection of valuable start-up resources for the budding entrepreneur. See if any catch your eye. You can order these books from your local bookstore, or call the company directly at:

The Oasis Press
(800) 228-2275

Before You Go Into Business, Read This

Realize your business potential and gain the know-how of business basics. Make starting your own business easier and less complicated.

Business Basics: A Microbusiness Start-up Guide

Its back-to-the-basics approach will help you handle the rigors of start-up with less muscle strain.

California Corporation Formation Package & Minute Book

All you Californians, pay attention! This book provides state-specific info on incorporation fees, deadlines, notices, regulations, elections, minutes, articles, and a whole bunch more.

College Entrepreneur Handbook

College is a great time to start a business! Take advantage of the opportunities and resources right on campus with this book's advice and insights.

Complete Book of Business Forms

A handy book that features ready-to-use forms for every area of running a business.

Develop & Market Your Creative Ideas: Bringing New Ideas to the Marketplace

Have a great idea but don't know where to go from there? Get things rolling with the info in this book — from trademarks, licensing, prototypes to distribution test marketing.

The Essential Corporation Handbook

A gotta-have-it book for anyone interested in incorporating a start-up. Learn about corporate formalities and the do's and don'ts. Get handy checklists and sample documents too.

The Essential Limited Liability Company Handbook

Get the scoop on one of the most recent forms of doing business — the LLC.

Home Business Made Easy

See if one of these 175 home-based, start-up biz ideas strikes your fancy.

Kick Ass Success: How to Achieve It

This book's fun to read and savvy all at the same time. An entertaining look at ways to make your biz prosper with tips on business management, selling, employees, and service.

Legal Road Map for Consultants

Maintain a safe and legal consulting biz with this informative guide on what to look out for, how to choose a good business lawyer, what to expect from the IRS, and other biz-related topics.

Location, Location, Location: How to Select the Best Site for Your Business

Guess what this book's about? Whether you're looking for a new biz site or relocating, increase your sales by choosing the right place — this book tells you what you need to know.

Moonlighting: Earn a Second Income at Home

If you're dreaming of running your own biz part-time or starting a home-based biz, then this book's worth its weight in gold.

Passion Rules! Inspiring Women in Business

Discover the power of passion through interviews with two dozen extraordinary American businesswomen, including diet guru Jenny Craig, PowerBar's Jennifer Maxwell, and Mrs. Field's Cookies' founder Debbie Fields Rose. In addition to recognizing passion as the driving force behind success and to encouraging you to identify and follow yours, this fascinating book offers solid, track-tested advice on such start-up business basics as setting goals, conducting feasibility studies, and networking. Also, there are sections devoted to business resources and support organizations.

Retail in Detail: How to Start and Manage a Small Retail Business

Tackle the retail world head on with this book. It features everything for going the distance — from choosing product lines and pricing to employee relations and store image.

SmartStart Your (State) Business series

A unique start-up guide for small business owners because of its one-stop, federal and state-specific info. It's all you need to know to start a business in your state. A must-have biz resource!

Which Business? Help in Selecting Your New Venture

Thinking about the best biz idea for yourself? If you need some help getting through all the hype to the real-deal info, this book's your ticket to making your decision.

You Can't Go Wrong By Doing It Right

Learn 50 terrific ways to go against the grain and create an overall positive attitude with customers and employees. This book holds the secret strategies for personalizing your start-up.

Notes

Plan of Action for Start-Up Issues

Your company will be a:
☐ Sole proprietorship   ☐ Partnership   ☐ Corporation   ☐ LLC

Use this planning tool to organize and prioritize the activities in this chapter that you've checked off. Don't feel you have to list all the activities you've checked off. Simply start with the top ten most important ones and go from there, or do whatever is easiest for you. Make plenty of copies of this cut-out worksheet for your planning and organizing activities for this chapter.

Action to be Taken	Begin Date	Who	Deadline

Plan of Action (continued)

Action to be Taken	Begin Date	Who	Deadline
_____	_____	_____	_____
_____	_____	_____	_____
_____	_____	_____	_____
_____	_____	_____	_____
_____	_____	_____	_____
_____	_____	_____	_____
_____	_____	_____	_____
_____	_____	_____	_____
_____	_____	_____	_____
_____	_____	_____	_____
_____	_____	_____	_____
_____	_____	_____	_____
_____	_____	_____	_____
_____	_____	_____	_____
_____	_____	_____	_____
_____	_____	_____	_____
_____	_____	_____	_____
_____	_____	_____	_____
_____	_____	_____	_____
_____	_____	_____	_____
_____	_____	_____	_____
_____	_____	_____	_____
_____	_____	_____	_____
_____	_____	_____	_____
_____	_____	_____	_____

Chapter 2

Money Matters

Introduction

Most of us want to start our own business to be independent and creative, but let's admit it, we also want the opportunity to make the big bucks — or at least enough to pay the bills! But whatever reason you have for getting into business, you won't stay in the game very long unless you have an independent source of financing. You've got to know how to get the money, maintain it, keep it flowing, and invest it.

Helping you understand your financial position is this chapter's goal. The first half of the chapter covers the issues and activities involved in funding your business, and the second half discusses everyday money matters for running a business. The checklists are designed to give you a basis for dealing with your company's finances and to raise any red flags that may keep you from succeeding.

Your new business will most likely cost you more money than you thought simply because most businesses soak up money in ways never dreamed of. Knowing this, and planning for your start-up and operational costs, will keep your head above water and may indeed, have you enjoying a profit.

First Aid for Money Matters

 The Oasis Press has a couple of very good books for getting funding and understanding the ways of the financial world — *Financing Your Small Business* by Art DeThomas and *Financial Decisionmaking: A Guide for the Non-Accountant* by David L. Fraley. Both books realize we're all not accountants and are written to help you understand all the mumbo-jumbo a banker or accountant can throw at you. These titles make creating and reading financials, getting a loan, and learning rule-of-thumb formulas as easy as possible. Check these titles out at your local bookstore or call up The Oasis Press directly. Either way, make sure you get some solid financial advice before opening your doors. In the long run, your efforts will pay off — hopefully in a big way!

Financial Decisionmaking: A Guide for the Non-Accountant
Financing Your Small Business   -
The Oasis Press
(800) 228-2275

Check out the Helpful Resources located at the end of this chapter for more tips on where to go for additional assistance regarding money matters.

Financing Your Business

You can finance your business in one of two ways — through equity or debt financing. Equity financing occurs when the owner sells interest in the business to outside investors who are interested in the business' potential growth. This type of financing is usually difficult to obtain for new start-ups because they have trouble proving their potential for exceptional growth and return on investment.

Debt financing will most likely be the most common way to finance your start-up. This financing occurs when you enter into a contractual agreement with a lender to repay the borrowed money, usually at a preset time, with interest. If payment is not received, the lender can take legal action against you to collect the amount that's owed.

Possibly the worst thing you can do when you start your business is to find out that you don't have enough money to run the business and to make a living from it. To keep this from happening, determine your financial needs before you start the business, know what your needs will be after the business is started, and how you'll get more money when needed.

Start-Up Financial Needs Checklist

First, think through all the expenses you'll incur to get started. As a new business owner, you'll often be required to make a full year's payment in advance or pay a deposit to obtain a lease or open an account with various suppliers, vendors, and utilities.

Do your figuring on a separate piece of paper, and use the items featured in this checklist as a starting point for estimating your start-up expenses and needs. Write down every start-up expense you can think of and be as thorough as possible. Research which items will require advance payment and estimate the amount you'll need for each expense you list.

Consider the following items:

☐ Office set-up needs. (Complete the Office Set-Up Checklist in Chapter 1.)

☐ Production equipment and supplies for producing your product.

☐ A business sign.

☐ The deposits you may have to pay to receive a necessary service or item. Think about:

    ☐ Electricity or natural gas services

    ☐ Office equipment

    ☐ Office furniture

    ☐ Rent or security deposits for your office space or building

    ☐ Telephone service hook up

    ☐ Water and sewer services

☐ Insurance needs.

☐ Business accounts you'll need to set up with others.

    What suppliers will you need and how do you set up accounts with them?

    Are there any account set-up fees?

    What will it cost to start a checking account for your business? What about getting a credit card for your business?

☐ Employee-related expenses. Consider:

    ☐ Payroll taxes

    ☐ Recruitment costs

    ☐ Training costs

☐ Wages and benefits

☐ Workers' compensation insurance

☐ Other start-up fees — such as licensing and registration fees. Refer to Chapter 1.

   ☐ Inventory items (and their costs) to ensure a good start in production, order fulfillment, or service performance.

☐ Initial advertising and marketing costs. Refer to Chapter 3.

What form of advertising do you want to use initially? A direct mail piece, newspaper ad, or flyer?

How much will it cost to produce the advertisement?

How much will it cost to distribute or run the advertisement?

What resources will be involved for tracking the ad's effectiveness?

☐ Your business license(s).

☐ Incorporating your business, if applicable.

☐ Franchise packages, if applicable.

☐ Lawyer and accountant services.

☐ Membership fees for trade and industry organizations and associations.

☐ Resource materials, such as how-to business books and business seminars.

Cash Needs Checklist

After determining your expenses, think about your income estimates for the first years following the opening of your business. You may find you don't need to go to a bank for a loan, but to know this, you'll need to do a cash-flow projection for the business.

Some lenders and consultants will refer to any financial sheet projections as "pro formas." This is a term used to designate future financial estimates for a business rather than basing figures on numbers from past experience. You can do pro formas for your future balance sheets, income statements, and cash-flow projections. These are valuable tools for determining your income estimates. Consider completing this activity with your financial adviser.

When trying to determine how much money it'll take to start your business, estimating your cash needs is an obvious step. You need to be as comprehensive and as thorough as possible when determining how much cash it will take to start your business.

☐ Estimate your personal cash needs for the coming three years.

    ☐ Look at your household budgets for the past couple of years, then determine what changes you expect in that budget for the coming years, after the business is up and running.

    What additional expenses do you see the business costing you personally?

    What's the estimated total of your personal expenses after the business opens?

☐ Use the information from the above activity to help you estimate the amount of salary or draw you'll need from the business to cover your personal expenses and to make a living.

☐ Estimate your sales from the business for the next three years.

☐ Prepare a pro forma cash-flow projection, income statement, and balance sheet for the next three years for the business. (See definitions in the Glossary.) Try to answer the following questions when preparing these reports:

    When do your business plan projections indicate you will be able to draw a salary from the business? How much will it be?

    How are you estimating your sales? Are you being optimistic or pessimistic?

    What changes will occur during the coming year that may affect your sales both negatively or positively?

☐ List the sources of cash you have available to you for the coming three years and specify how much money you can count on from them.

_____

_____

_____

_____

_____

    Will these sources influence your cash-flow projection?

    Are these sources reliable?

    Can these sources of income lead you to additional sources?

Going to a Lender Checklist

Once you realize what your start-up and cash needs will be, you may be looking for a new source of funding — and that means making a trip to a lender. This checklist — based on *The Insider's Guide to Small Business Loans* by Dan Koehler — is about getting ready for this match up by having you consider which type of lender you need and being well-prepared when applying for a start-up, small business loan.

- [ ] If you're interested in short-term debt funding, the following sources are available to you:

  - [ ] Your own commercial bank
  - [ ] Commercial finance companies
  - [ ] Factoring companies (See Glossary for definitions.)
  - [ ] Small Business Investment Companies (SBICs)
  - [ ] State and local economic development programs
  - [ ] U.S. Small Business Administration (SBA)

- [ ] If you're interested in long-term financing, check out the following possibilities:

  - [ ] Commercial banks
  - [ ] Commercial finance companies
  - [ ] Equipment manufacturers
  - [ ] Independent leasing companies
  - [ ] Life insurance companies
  - [ ] Savings and loan institutions
  - [ ] U.S. Small Business Administration
  - [ ] Venture capitalists

- [ ] Investigate the possibility of offering the sale of common stock or securities for your business.

  - [ ] Contact the Securities and Exchange Commission (SEC) for more information on securities laws.

- [ ] When you go to a lender for a start-up loan, be able to:

  - [ ] Specify the amount you need.
  - [ ] Indicate the amount of cash you're willing to put into the venture.
  - [ ] Show how you'll successfully manage your start-up.
  - [ ] Prove you have the collateral necessary to support the loan.

☐ Anticipate the following aspects to the loan:

    ☐ The monthly payment amount

    ☐ Possible increases in the payments

    ☐ Processing time

    ☐ Closing costs

☐ Financial information and documents to have in your hands include:

    ☐ Copies of your personal income tax returns for at least the previous three years, and a personal financial statement.

    ☐ Pro forma balance sheets and income statements for at least one year.

    ☐ A comprehensive, financing proposal.

    ☐ A well-prepared, professional business plan package (See Chapter 7 for the nitty gritty details.)

    ☐ Projected cash-flow statements for at least three years into future.

    ☐ Related documentation, such as letters of support, testimonials, company literature, or photographs, or prototypes of product.

☐ Educate yourself as much as possible on the loan process. Be well-prepared and knowledgeable before you even walk in the lender's door.

Finding the Right Banker Checklist

If you choose and develop a relationship with a bank before you open your doors, you'll have a much better chance of getting the financing you need when the time comes. That's why it's a good idea to do some bank shopping now. Find out which bank in town offers you the best bang for your buck. Treat them like you would any other vendor — expect quality service at good prices.

Once you decide on a bank, you'll be more comfortable learning about banking terms, types of loans, and financial statements and services. This checklist, and the book, *The Small Business Insider's Guide to Bankers*, will get you headed in the right direction for choosing the best bank for your new business.

☐ Research the local phone directory to make a list of the banks nearest you.

☐ Determine if you're interested in a large or small bank by investigating:

    ☐ Respective services;

    ☐ Cost of services; and

    ☐ Convenience, such as multi-branches, access to loans, and loan types.

☐ Set up get-to-know-each-other interviews with each bank's small business department or loan officer.

   ☐ Have a one- or two-page synopsis of your business to leave with the banker.

   ☐ Be honest and open during the interview.

   ☐ Consider bringing projected financials with you to discuss.

   ☐ Inquire about what the bank requires for small business loan requests.

☐ Interview financial institutions to see which ones are willing to give you the most for your business. Some questions to ask during this interview could include:

How can you reduce checking costs?

Can you transfer money from interest-bearing accounts to checking accounts by phone?

Will you get free cashier's checks or money orders?

Can you get reduced fees for cashing international checks or other instruments, such as a letter of credit?

☐ Compare checking account services and fees.

   ☐ Ask about the bank's monthly, per-check, and account analysis charges for its checking services.

☐ Find out about its services and fees for the following:

   ☐ Equipment loans

   ☐ International money transfers

   ☐ Inventory loans

   ☐ Overdrafts

   ☐ Returned checks

☐ Check out potential investment opportunities at the bank.

If your company generates enough extra cash, can you invest in real estate or mutual funds?

What are your options for investing surplus cash without tying it up?

☐ Inquire about floor plan financing, accounts receivable financing, and lines of credit as available options for your business. See the Glossary for definitions of each.

☐ If you plan to build a plant or retail store, you will need a construction loan before the permanent financing. See if the bank provides both forms of financing.

☐ Ask about credit card arrangements with the bank for various credit card companies.

☐ Be sure to ask about charge-back procedures on all the credit cards you are considering signing up for. Different card companies have different policies regarding your ability to protest a charge and how they will deal with crediting you for overcharges and errors in your billing.

Everyday Business Money Matters

Many consultants say the primary cause of business failure is lack of funding. If that's true, then a close second is because an owner doesn't pay enough attention to the ongoing financial condition of the company and operates on a crisis-management basis. He waits until bills are due before realizing that funds are not available to pay them, which is usually not the best time to seek financial help. Additionally, knowing where your money is going so that you can plug unnecessary leaks of cash will add to your profit and prevent undue crises.

This section will remind you of some of the basic everyday money matters that will affect your cash flow. Hopefully, these areas are ones you have already thought about in your estimating of cash needs and listing of start-up expenses. If not, let the checklists in this section serve as helpers for getting you to think about or budget for various business items that can slip through the cracks when first starting a business.

Credit Policy and Collection Techniques Checklist

Extending the credit is easy; but there are definite risks involved. Collecting the money can be difficult. If you decide to extend credit, first develop your company's credit policy and think about ways to collect any overdue accounts. There's no right or wrong credit policy or collection technique; every small business is unique and faces different challenges.

The checklist below features general credit and collection tips and activities that can help you get organized in these areas. If you'd like more information on credit and collection, refer to The Oasis Press book, *Collection Techniques for a Small Business*.

- ☐ Determine whether your business will be financially able to offer credit or if it'll need to operate on a cash-only basis.

- ☐ If you extend credit, develop a credit policy that includes the following information:

  - ☐ Consider the amount of deposit you'll accept and how you'll want the remainder of money owed to be paid, for example, cash only or by billing the customer.

  - ☐ Decide if you'll accept checks, and if so, determine your process and what identifications or verifications you'll require.

  - ☐ Decide if you'll accept credit cards, and if so, choose which ones you'll accept, and how you'll conduct credit checks.

  - ☐ Detail your credit terms, such as discounts for early payment or penalties for late payments.

  - ☐ Indicate what it'll take for a customer or supplier to qualify for credit.

  - ☐ Create a new client (supplier) questionnaire to help you gather important information on potential creditors.

- ☐ Once you develop a credit policy, explain it thoroughly to all your employees to ensure consistency.

- ☐ Anticipate what it'll cost to run credit checks and include the cost in any preplanning budget.

- ☐ To help collect any debt effectively, consider the following key principles regarding collection techniques:

  - ☐ Follow up within five days after a payment is due. Be sure to check that day's mail before calling.

  - ☐ Set up your own follow-up system for collecting debts, and always be consistent in your follow up.

  - ☐ Develop a strong recordkeeping system to keep track of your phone conversations and written correspondence regarding debt collection.

  - ☐ Treat a debtor in a friendly, respectful manner on the first couple of contacts.

  - ☐ Be careful to follow the legal and ethical guidelines for debt collecting. For example, do not harass a debtor or make an effort to ruin his reputation.

  - ☐ Always ask for payment in full, but be ready and willing to suggest partial payment alternatives and be flexible with any alternatives offered by the debtor.

☐ Motivate and work with the debtor to help her pay the debt by appealing to basic human needs, such as pride, honor, and integrity.

☐ Try to maintain your customer's or supplier's goodwill while you work on getting your money.

Recordkeeping Checklist

Keeping track of all your financial statements, reports, and notices will keep you out of hot water with your state revenue department and the IRS — not to mention, make it easier for you to stay on top of your everyday money matters.

☐ Choose the person responsible for doing your financial records.

Will this be the same person who will do your payroll?

Will this person be responsible for preparing all payroll reports, such as for FUTA, income tax withholdings, FICA, and workers' compensation?

☐ Consider if a fiscal year end or calendar year end is more advantageous for your business.

☐ Determine the kind of accounting system you'll use in your business.

If you have a personal computer, what type of software package best fits your needs? Be sure to compare and shop around.

If you don't have a personal computer, what type of hand accounting system will you use?

☐ Choose the person responsible for completing reports for reasons such as:

☐ Reports to banks or financial institutions;

☐ Taxes for local, state, federal governments; and

☐ Corporate reports to state and federal governments.

Business Insurance Checklist

The checklist below, which is based on The Oasis Press book, *The Buyer's Guide to Business Insurance*, by Don Bury and Larry Heischman, gives an outline of basic prepurchase items you can do to make your business insurance purchase an economical and comprehensive one.

☐ Gather information about your business and its insurance needs and use it to streamline the quote process and get the most coverage for your dollar. Information to gather includes:

- [ ] A general company history, if any; and a thorough description of your current or projected operations; and annual projected payroll, sales or receipts;
- [ ] Copies of existing insurance policies, leases, and marketing and business plans;
- [ ] Copies of loss runs from insurance companies if you're purchasing an existing business;
- [ ] The dates you want all of your policies to begin and expire;
- [ ] Information about and descriptions of such items as the buildings you occupy (even if you rent), machinery and equipment, and employee-owned property on your premises (like a mechanic's tools);
- [ ] A list of all vehicles used in the business; include the year, make, model, cost new, use of each unit, and the distance they are driven on a normal day; and
- [ ] Copies of your driving records, and those of any family members who drive your business vehicles, and those of all your employees.

- [ ] Get to know what types of insurance sellers there are in the insurance industry's marketplace, as well as their respective duties and specialties.

  - [ ] Choose several well-educated, experienced agents or brokers, or both, with whom to shop for your purchase. Ask for referrals from your friendly competitors; your national, state, or local associations; or your chamber of commerce.
  - [ ] Try to build a favorable rapport with insurance sellers as you work to reduce your price and increase service.
  - [ ] Find out how insurance companies are rated and how financially stable they are.
  - [ ] Learn the difference between an admitted and a nonadmitted insurance company.
  - [ ] Select the insurance companies you want to insure your business.

- [ ] Know your business insurance coverage options by familiarizing yourself with the following:

  - [ ] Determine if you should insure all of your vehicles or not.

    What does the state and your bank require?
    Do you need physical damage on all of them?

☐ Investigate commercial general liability insurance, which protects you from lawsuits from incidents, such as injuries to the general public on your business' premises.

☐ Determine the practicality of coverage for earthquakes, flood, building ordinances and laws, glass, and pollution.

☐ Know the difference between replacement cost versus actual cash value.

☐ Ask about coverage for any property in transit or any special equipment that might break down, and, as a result, jeopardize the entire operation.

☐ Determine if you want special coverage for your computer system.

☐ Determine costs for coverage for theft losses from employees.

☐ Familiarize yourself on coverage for loss of business income caused by a loss to your property.

☐ Compare deductibles to the amount of savings in premium.

☐ Consider whether or not you will need a bond to secure a license or contract.

☐ Once you investigate all the different types of available insurance coverage, work with your agents and brokers to compile your coverage checklist.

☐ When negotiating price, remember:

☐ Agents and brokers don't get paid unless you buy from them, thus putting you in an excellent position to negotiate.

☐ An informed buyer with her information well-compiled is empowered to shop easily and deserves and demands the best possible price and service.

☐ The agent or broker gets his commission out of your purchase price.

☐ Check if the insurance company offers an installment payment plan. This may be less expensive and more convenient than paying the premium up front, or using outside premium financing.

Financial Management Checklist

If you plan to start a one- or two-person operation, the idea of financial management may seem unnecessary for your business preplanning. Simply doing your own books or hiring an accountant may be as far as you want to plan at first; however, once your business begins to grow, financial management will and should become an important part of your responsibilities.

This checklist gives a brief overview of the factors it'll take to manage your company's finances. *Bottom Line Basics*, by Robert Low, is an excellent resource on financial management.

- [ ] Develop at least a one-year projection for your company, broken down by months, that includes:
    - [ ] A balance sheet;
    - [ ] A cash-flow statement;
    - [ ] An income statement; and
    - [ ] A 13-week cash-flow forecast, broken down by weeks, if needed.

- [ ] Use this projection to determine:
    - [ ] How much financing you require;
    - [ ] Your break-even level of sales; and
    - [ ] The impact on profits of different levels of sales and expenses.

- [ ] Monitor actual performance against the plan.
    - [ ] Revise the plan as needed.

- [ ] Automate your accounting system.
    - [ ] Determine the type of software needed.
    - [ ] Determine how often formal financial statements are needed.
    - [ ] Establish a deadline to have monthly financial statements finished by the seventh working day of the following month and take time to analyze the results.

- [ ] Develop daily or weekly flash reports that capture key business indicators.
    - [ ] These indicators may include nonfinancial measures, such as number of sales leads, percent of capacity used, or units produced.

- [ ] Focus on cash flow.
    - [ ] Establish credit policies and follow up promptly on past due accounts.
    - [ ] Maximize inventory turnover and monitor the levels and salability of stock on hand.

- [ ] Establish internal controls that ensure separation of duties for transactions, especially cash disbursements.
    - [ ] Create logs for sales orders, purchase orders, invoices, and shipments.

☐ Have all cash accounts reconciled monthly.

☐ Always verify your signature on all outgoing checks to avoid potential embezzlement.

☐ Calculate your costs and determine target profit margins.

Are you charging enough for your products or services?

How much do you charge to cover overhead expenses, such as space, support staff, and equipment?

At what markup will you be able to pay all fixed and variable costs?

☐ Clarify the roles of your key accounting and finance people, such as your bookkeeper, accountant, controller, and certified public accountant.

☐ Retain the services of a good financial adviser to help you in your financial management preplanning process.

Tax-Saving Tips Checklist

One way you can help your new start-up succeed in money matters is to begin developing tax-saving strategies before you even open your doors. Be prepared to deal with the new, methodical tax rules of the business game. This checklist is based on the business guide, *Top Tax Saving Ideas for Today's Small Business*, written by Thomas Stemmy, and can be used as a starting point for educating and familiarizing yourself with ways to plan for and save on your taxes.

☐ Understand the tax advantages and disadvantages of the legal form of business you choose for your business, for example, sole proprietorship or corporation.

☐ Educate yourself on what the IRS considers as a legitimate business write-off.

☐ Discover how fringe benefits to employees can prove to be valuable tax advantages.

☐ Know when and how much to pay on your estimated income taxes so you can avoid possible penalties and interest.

☐ Don't take business deductions for granted; you, alone, are responsible for providing proof that you're entitled to the write-off. To help do this:

☐ Claim your deductions in the right year.

☐ Pay by check whenever possible and keep receipts of cash transactions.

☐ Record all business mileage and telephone usage.

☐ Investigate how income-splitting could be of benefit to your tax strategy.

☐ Familiarize yourself with the new tax rules by reading updated tax publications or discussing them with your accountant or certified public accountant.

☐ Get professional advice on how to do estate planning in connection with one of your most important assets — your business operations. Secure a future for you and your family and receive tax savings at the same time.

☐ Determine what retirement planning and tax deferrals you can implement into your tax-saving strategies. Possible options include:

    ☐ Individual retirement accounts (IRAs)

    ☐ Keogh plans

    ☐ Profit-sharing and pension plans

    ☐ Simplified Employee Pension (SEP) plans

☐ Stay abreast of current tax-saving trends by regularly meeting with your accountant, reading business magazines, attending business tax seminars, and visiting tax-related web sites.

Strategies and Tips

From knowing what it'll cost you to open your doors to knowing how to manage your finances, preplanning is the key to helping you through the money matters aspect of the business game. It cannot be emphasized enough that you need to have a clear understanding of your financial position *before* starting your business. Take the information you have gleaned from this chapter, and work on your Plan of Action for Money Matters worksheet.

- Make a smart move in the business game and get a strong, savvy accountant who's well-experienced and qualified in preparing financials and dealing with small business.

- To see if a bank has a good track record on requested loans, get annual or quarterly statements of the bank and check the loan-to-deposit ratio. Banks that are the most active lenders will have a ratio of around 55 to 75 percent.

- Having a well-prepared business plan is one of the main ingredients for starting a loan application process.

- Consider having an outside professional do your payroll checks. Unless you know what you're doing, the IRS may come to call.

- Keep insurance costs low with consistent negotiating. The squeaky wheel gets the grease.

- Banks won't lend to people who only have vague ideas of what they want and need. So do your homework before going to the bank.

- Be as conservative as possible when budgeting for your start-up expenses. Start small, and buy as you grow.

- Banks are relying on cash-flow projections more now than ever. And they'll want the estimates to be backed up with supporting information and documents and reasonable estimates.

- Commercial banks rank as the largest single source of extended-term financing for small businesses.

- Be honest with your banker. If you have a problem, let the banker know before the word spreads on the streets.

- Don't overlook the possibility of obtaining a loan through the U.S. Small Business Administration. While many entrepreneurs think a business must be a minority-owned one to qualify for SBA financing, this is not the case.

- Cash flow refers to how you obtain your cash, not your sales. There is a major difference between cash and credit, and how cash flows into your business will determine if you stay in business.

- A well-defined, well-written credit policy will make your future customers feel that you treat all customers equally.

Helpful Resources

Here are some financial resources to consider. For more of the same, you can refer to the appendices in the back of the book for info on SBDCs, biz magazines and other publications, and online resources for small business.

American Bankers Association (ABA)
(800) 338-0626

Call for information on available bankers and how-to finance advice.

422 Tax Deductions for Businesses & Self-Employed Individuals
Bell Springs Publishing
(800) 515-8050

Get all the deductions you deserve once your start-up is off and running. Check out all these legitimate write-offs and save big!

The Frugal Entrepreneur: Creative Ways to Save Time, Energy and Money in Your Business
Portico Press
(800) 222-7656

This upbeat, practical collection of tips and techniques will save you tons of money in running your biz. It's brimming with all sorts of saving secrets.

Money Smart Secrets for the Self-Employed
Random House
(800) 726-0600

Here are some insider tips for being your own boss and making a living at it too!

National Association of Government Guaranteed Lenders (NAGGL)
(405) 377-4022

A good resource for finding funding from the government.

The Small Business Guide to Borrowing Money
Bell Springs Publishing
(800) 515-8050

Here are some sources of funding that you may never have known about or considered, plus you'll learn how to prepare a top-notch loan application and get the best terms.

Start Up Financing
Career Press
(800) 227-3371

A good resource for finding and getting the money you'll need to get the biz ball rolling.

Helpful Resources from The Oasis Press

The Oasis Press — The Leading Publisher of Small Business Information also has a collection of valuable financial resources for the budding entrepreneur. See if any catch your eye. You can order these books from your local bookstore, or call the company directly at:

The Oasis Press
(800) 228-2275

Bottomline Basics: Understand & Control Business Finances

A good beginner's book for getting your financial management feet wet.

Business Owner's Guide to Accounting and Bookkeeping

Get your money books and statements in tip-top shape with this easy, how-to regime.

businessplan.com

Nope, this isn't a web site — this book's on the cutting edge with its advice on how to gather and research info from the Internet to write a knock-out business plan.

The Buyer's Guide to Business Insurance

A step-by-step guide featuring tips on how to improve your biz insurance costs, coverage, and service.

Collection Techniques for Small Business

From establishing a credit policy to preparing for small claims courts, the book helps you avoid bad debts and collection problems.

Financial Decisionmaking: A Guide for the Non-Accountant

This book translates the language of finance into plain English. Understanding cash flow, financial statements, debt, and stock pricing and other money topics becomes much easier.

Financial Management Techniques for Small Business

This financial resource will help you keep tabs on your financial situation's ups and downs. Learn how to interpret figures and detect potential problems with this book and software package.

Financing Your Small Business: Techniques for Planning, Acquiring & Managing Debt

Identify, approach, attract, and manage sources of financing with the tricks and techniques outlined by a savvy money manager.

Funding High-Tech Ventures

Discover an insider's proven strategies for getting your state-of-the-art biz idea off the starting line with funding, product development, and marketing.

Insider's Guide to Small Business Loans

Get some tips on simplifying the loan process, preparing the loan application, and dealing with the Small Business Administration.

Legal Expense Defense: How to Control Your Business' Legal Costs and Problems

Take charge of your legal costs and do more legal work in-house with this book. There's reproducible forms and worksheets to boot.

The Rule Book of Business Plans for Startups

A business plan book just for start-ups! Learn the unique "rules" for structuring, compiling, and writing your start-up business plan so you get the dollars you need. Along the way, discover your strengths and weaknesses and use your plan to overcome potential pitfalls.

The Small Business Insider's Guide to Bankers

A great source for ways to meet the right banker and get the funding you need from them. Learn what they're looking for and what you need to bring to make it all happen.

Top Tax Saving Ideas for Today's Small Business

Get tax-savvy and tax-savings with this concise, friendly guide for the start-up and existing biz.

Write Your Own Business Contracts: What Your Attorney Won't Tell You

Draft your own contracts before going to your attorney and save some bucks and time with this how-to legal guide.

Plan of Action for Money Matters

Your company will hire an:

☐ In-house accountant ☐ Accounting consultant

Use this planning tool to organize and prioritize the activities in this chapter that you've checked off. Don't feel you have to list all the activities you've checked off. Simply start with the top ten most important ones and go from there, or do whatever is easiest for you. Make plenty of copies of this cut-out worksheet for your planning and organizing activities for this chapter.

Action to be Taken	Begin Date	Who	Deadline

Plan of Action (continued)

Action to be Taken	Begin Date	Who	Deadline

Chapter 3

Marketing Strategies

Introduction

If you've ever played or watched chess before, then you know about the concentration and strategizing that goes on before a move is made. One wrong move, and checkmate! Well, the same goes for playing the business game. If you miss a smart marketing move, you could miss out on valuable sales and public relations opportunities.

When it comes to strategizing your new start-up's marketing plan, focusing on your marketing message and moves will increase your chances for more sales and profit. To do this, however, will take some time and research, but in the long run, you'll be glad you made the effort. To begin:

- Determine your target market.
- Test market your produce or service.
- Understand your advertising options and marketing budget needs.

By giving some thought and research to these activities, you're more likely to spend your marketing dollar more effectively. You'll be more focused on getting your message out and creating a company image that'll set you apart from your competition.

That's why this chapter takes you through the activities necessary for initial market research, marketing communications strategies, marketing plans and budgets.

First Aid for Marketing Strategies

Most of the information and activities listed in Chapter 3 are based on *Power Marketing for Small Business*, written by Jody Hornor. If you need a basic, all-in-one marketing book to help you learn about marketing in general, then this book's for you. You'll find it extremely valuable in completing all of the activities mentioned in this chapter. Another valuable marketing book you may find helpful is *Marketing Mastery: Your Seven Step Guide to Success*, written by Harriet Stephenson and Dorothy Otterson.

You can obtain a copy of these books in any local bookstore, or order directly from the publisher.

Marketing Mastery: Your Seven Step Guide to Success
Power Marketing for Small Business
The Oasis Press
(800) 228-2275

Other valuable sales and marketing resources, including a Plan of Action for Marketing Strategies worksheet are listed at the end of this chapter.

Market Research

Remember when you wrote a high school research paper or a detailed analysis or report for your employer? Before you handed in the final paper, you had to roll up your sleeves and do some research on the subject. The same principle applies when developing a marketing strategy for your business.

With a marketing plan, learn who your target market is, what that market needs and how it buys, and how your product or service stands out in the crowd. Don't be daunted by the prospect of spending some time in the library, on the phone or Internet, or with an adviser. Look at it as a treasure hunt. Every bit of data and information you discover will lead you closer to your pot of gold — a successful and prosperous business.

Don't underestimate the importance of market research in your marketing strategy. Market research focuses you on the long term and is designed to closely support both strategic marketing and product planning. Go at it with enthusiasm and focus. Use the checklists in this section to give you an idea of what you'll need to research.

Target Market Checklist

Targeting your market means understanding very specifically who your prospective customers will be and why they'll be coming your way. To discover who your target customer is, you'll need to study demographics.

☐ Determine the demographic profile of your target market. To collect demographic data, you can use:

    ☐ A survey with in-person questionnaires or conduct a survey by phone;

    ☐ Private research firms;

    ☐ Trade and professional associations;

    ☐ U.S. Bureau of the Census data; and

    ☐ U.S. Small Business Administration materials.

☐ Determine the psychographic profile of the people most likely to purchase your product or service. To collect psychographic data, use the options listed above. In addition, consider:

    Who or what influences your target market in its buying decisions? How does your market shop for and buy similar products or services?

    Are your market's attitudes, values, or habits changing? If so, how?

☐ Write a description of your target market after you've determined its demographics and psychographics. Ask yourself these questions as you complete this aspect of your market research:

    Is the product or service you offer geared to a consumer or business prospect?

    Can everyone in that consumer or business group use your product, or is there a particular type of business or individual that's more apt to purchase it?

    Does age, sex, income level, or lifestyle of the business or individual indicate a more qualified prospect?

☐ Divide your target market into market segments if the target market is too large for you to reach with your budget or the available marketing media.

Product or Service Checklist

Once you know who your target market is and what motivates it to buy, consider how your product or service is unique, why it's appealing, and how you can get feedback on your product or service so you know if it's feasible to go ahead with your marketing plans.

☐ List all your product's or service's strengths and weaknesses.

_____

_____

_____

_____

_____

_____

_____

☐ List all your product's or service's physical features or aspects and all of the benefits it provides to customers.

_____

_____

_____

_____

_____

_____

_____

☐ List all of your competitors and their strengths and weaknesses.

_____

_____

_____

_____

_____

_____

☐ Compare your product or service to those of your competitors, and assess how you stand out from the rest.

☐ Note any unique features or benefits you offer over those of your competitors so you can use this position in your marketing strategies.

☐ Create a catchy, five-to-seven word slogan that captures this position.

☐ Test market your product or service to determine its most appropriate price, packaging, and shipping methods. Keep in mind:

> Can you sell your product or service for a price that's profitable?
>
> Are the attributes of your product or service desirable and saleable?
>
> Which packaging encourages the most sales?
>
> What constitutes a successful test market? By what criteria will you judge your results?
>
> How are you going to track your results?
>
> Which variable will you test first, second, third? Never test market two variables at the same time, you cannot track results.

☐ Compare your price with those of your competitors to see if it's reasonable and workable in your market.

☐ Compare your price with the price of producing the product or providing the service.

☐ Specify any guarantees or warranties you'll offer.

> How do they compare with your competitors?
>
> Will they be limited guarantees or warranties?
>
> How will a warranty affect your price?

☐ Research any buying objections your target market may have regarding your product or service.

> How can you overcome these buying objections?
>
> Will any solutions require product modifications or a change in your marketing message?

☐ Ensure your product packaging is professional and appropriate.

> Does the package represent the business in the way you want it to be perceived?
>
> Is the packaging cost-effective?
>
> Is the packaging environment-friendly?

☐ Ensure the packaging for your service is professional and represents the company well.

Market Research Sources and Techniques

Trying to figure out where to start and how to conduct your market research for your target market and product or service can seem pretty overwhelming at first. But thanks to several leading marketing experts and consultants, there are many how-to, self-help marketing books available. *Know Your Market: How to Do Low-Cost Market Research* by David B. Frigstad is one of these helpful publications.

In his book, Mr. Frigstad explains how you can obtain primary and secondary sources of information, as well as various techniques for researching marketing and sales issues, all of which can help you either write your own marketing plan or set up your company's market information system (MIS). An MIS is when you organize procedures and methods that will gather market information on an ongoing and regular basis. A discussion of what to include in a marketing plan occurs later in this chapter.

So, to help you get out of the starting blocks and up and running with your market research — which is an extremely important role in the business game — this section features a couple of checklists that are based upon the information presented in *Know Your Market*.

Market Research Sources Checklist

Primary research is obtained by gathering information directly from a consumer, supplier, or competitor and is vital to any research project's completion. Secondary research, however, is aimed more at familiarizing a researcher with an industry's technology, jargon, and trends and is used more to complement a research project rather than complete one.

☐ Before beginning any research project, outline all the details you wish to cover. For instance:

    ☐ Determine how long the forecast period will be for your various marketing aspects, including sales forecasts or technological trends.

    ☐ Decide what to include in the forecast, such as pricing considerations.

    ☐ Identify potential markets and note all product applications, including market application segments, end-user segments, and geographic segments.

    ☐ Identify the fields of technology you need to analyze.

    ☐ Consider which competitors to analyze and exactly what information you'll want to gather about each one.

☐ Define what type of information you want regarding the end-user of your product or service.

☐ Once you know what research information you need, select which primary data collection method you'll use. Primary research collection methods include:

☐ Mail surveys or questionnaires

☐ Personal interviews

☐ Telephone interviews

☐ Research how to effectively conduct your interviews or surveys.

☐ Develop the questionnaires for your survey or interview.

☐ Gather as many external secondary sources as possible. Consider using:

☐ Associations pertaining to your business or trade;

☐ Computerized bibliographies or online services;

☐ Government agencies and publications; and

☐ Public library reference desks.

☐ Consider attending industry trade shows to gather preliminary market information on such topics as marketing strategies, product information, competitors, customer interest levels, and technical trends.

☐ Educate yourself on the basics of sales forecasting and how it can help you project sales figures and be a vital part of your market research.

Competitor Research Techniques Checklist

When you research competitors, you gain a better understanding of how they stand in the marketplace, what their strategies are, and how their moves can affect your biz. Knowing what your competitors are doing in the marketplace will give you a decided advantage in the marketing game.

☐ Investigate your competitors in the following areas:

☐ Company organization

☐ Cost structure

☐ Distribution channels

☐ Financial position

☐ Management structure and style

☐ Product line

☐ Research and development

☐ Assess your competitors' objectives, including their financial, technical, market leadership, and general performance objectives.

☐ Identify the underlying beliefs of your competition by understanding how they perceive themselves, the market in general, and their competition.

☐ Focus on how your competitors operate.

What markets or niches do your competitors appear to concentrate on, and how do they compete in those markets? For example, is the competitor competing primarily on the basis of price, or is it focusing on technological differentiation of products?

☐ Consider the following sources for gathering competitor information:

☐ Company interviews

☐ Company literature

☐ End-user history

☐ Government filings

☐ Number of employees

☐ Plant inspections

☐ Visual observations

Market Analysis Techniques Checklist

Generally, no one market analysis technique is better than the other, and an ideal approach to this aspect of your research project would be to combine some or all of the methods mentioned in this checklist.

☐ Do a preliminary sales analysis of your company by doing sales forecasting or reviewing any existing sales records.

☐ Learn about the life cycle of your product or service and how each stage of the cycle will affect your price and position within your marketplace.

☐ Analyze how to price your product or service by evaluating your projected sales figures, the life cycle stage of your product or service, and your position in the marketplace.

☐ Evaluate ways you'll gain a larger share of your target market.

☐ Research new trends in technology that'll affect your market.

Marketing Communications Strategies

Once you know who your target market is, why your product or service is unique, and how you compare against your competitors, it's time to ask: "How will you let your target market know about your product or service?"

To educate your target market about your product or service, you'll need to "talk" to your market. This is where marketing communications comes into play. It's through marketing communications — public relations, advertising, and sales — that you're able to get your message out to your target market, get its attention, and eventually get its business. As a new business owner, simply getting a feel for marketing communications is a step in the right direction. The checklists in this section will not only do this for you, but they'll also make you think about details and information to incorporate into your first marketing communications strategy.

This section points out how you can utilize these marketing communications options and raise some issues and activities that'll move you towards a strong marketing strategy.

Public Relations Checklist

Public relations helps you create and manage a business image through newspapers, radio, and television with little or no cost. You submit newsworthy information about your business so they in turn publish or broadcast a story about you to your market. PR lays the groundwork for marketing, advertising, and sales by creating awareness and rapport with a marketplace.

This checklist, and The Oasis Press book, *Public Relations Marketing: Making a Splash Without Much Cash*, shows you how to develop your own public relations strategy.

☐ List all the media — newspapers, radio, and television stations — in your local area, plus any other media that would be interested in your product or service.

 Is there a national trade magazine that covers your industry or an out-of-state or local radio station that has a talk show applicable to your industry?

Does your local newspaper have a regular business section where you can send newsworthy information regarding your product or service?

☐ Make sure your media list includes the medium's name, contact person, mailing address, and phone number. Also note a medium's reach or circulation and any editorial material it reviews.

☐ Request a media kit from each of the mediums on your list. See the Glossary for a definition on media kits.

☐ From their media kits, see which of the media reaches your target market and disregard the rest.

☐ Recognize what a newsworthy event is for most media. Events, such as opening a new business, promoting an employee, or honors or awards achieved, will usually get a mention in the local media.

☐ Learn how to write an effective news release.

☐ Create a start-up public relations calendar for the first six-months of operation.

What company events or activities would be of interest to the local, regional, or national media? New hires? New product introduction? Your grand opening?

What months will these events and activities be occurring in?

☐ Designate who will write the news release, organize the mailing, and do the follow up.

☐ Join your local chamber of commerce, local business organizations, or become involved with community projects and events. Networking is a valuable part of any public relations program.

Internet Checklist

Besides working with traditional media sources to develop your PR strategy, you can also include the World Wide Web in your plan. The Internet is fast becoming one of the best ways to further manage company image. The book, *Connecting Online: Creating a Successful Image on the Internet,* is a terrific source for this aspect of an effective marketing communications strategy. Here's a sampling of the tips it provides.

☐ If you're not online already, get online and start learning how to surf the Net and navigate using your browser program. See how others are using the Internet and email.

☐ Determine what your goal for being on the Internet will be.

Do you have a weak brand or company name that needs a boost?

Is your service particularly unique and needs to be touted?

☐ Determine your target online audience.

☐ Create a few key messages that you want people to remember about your biz. Keep them simple and direct to avoid confusion.

☐ Select strategies and actions (such as a special event or new product) that will be worthy of news releases to be released over the Internet.

☐ Budget for online public relations expenses.

What hardware and software will you need?

What other outside costs will you have besides Internet Service Provider (ISP) costs?

☐ Explore online press release distribution services, discussion groups, and email processes.

☐ Discover how Usenet (newsgroups or net news) contributes to your online PR strategy.

☐ Research and design a web site. (You could write a book on this one, so check out *Connecting Online* for ways to do the job right.)

Advertising Checklist

Advertising is an integral part of any marketing communications strategy because you can reach so many different media sources to get your message out to a large number of people. Finding the right mix of these sources is the trickier part of the planning. To get a general feel for what steps you'll need to take, review this checklist and *Advertising Without An Agency: A Comprehensive Guide*.

☐ Write down what messages you want your target market to hear.

_____

_____

_____

_____

_____

_____

Are you unknown in the market? If so, your message may be to simply generate awareness of your product or service and establish some credibility — you don't want to close a sale by offering a discount.

☐ Ensure your advertising message recognizes both the needs of a prospective customer and the typical time frame in which he's likely to act by either purchasing or inquiring about your product or service.

If you have a new product, it'll take longer for a customer to respond. Your message shouldn't be geared towards closing a sale, but rather, it should focus on gaining the attention of your market.

☐ Once you have a clear idea of what messages to send, determine all your company's communications goals. For example:

　☐ Create awareness of your company, product, or service.

　☐ Educate the market about who you are and what you do.

　☐ Position the company against a major competitor.

☐ Check off the potential media sources below you'd consider buying advertising from. Some of your media options include:

☐ Billboard/outdoor advertising	☐ Newspapers
☐ Cooperative advertising	☐ Radio
☐ Direct mail	☐ Signs
☐ Directories	☐ Specialty advertising
☐ Magazines	☐ Television
☐ Newsletters	☐ Yellow Pages

☐ Request a media kit from each media source you might be interested in using.

☐ Review each media kit to discover the medium's total audience reach, that audience's demographics, and what the medium charges for ads.

☐ Calculate the cost-per-qualified contact by simply dividing the number of qualified prospects the medium reaches by how much it will cost you to advertise with that medium.

☐ Make a list of all the media that most effectively reaches your target audience for the least amount of money.

Optional Media Strategies and Research Checklist

Learn as much as possible about the media and what's available to you. The more you know, the better prepared you'll be for your business' marketing needs and efforts. The checklist below is designed to get you thinking about how you'll approach working with the media.

☐ Investigate any opportunities you may have for co-op advertising.

Do you have any regional or national suppliers that offer co-op advertising? If so, give them a call.

Would you be interested in starting your own co-op advertising?

☐ Develop a sample direct mail program to get a better feel for how economical and valuable this marketing communications strategy is for small businesses. To start:

☐ Purchase a mailing list of qualified or target customers.

☐ Decide on the type of direct mail piece you wish to send. For example:

☐ A post card

☐ A four-color piece

☐ A one-sheet advertisement with a discount coupon attached

☐ Estimate how much your postage will cost.

☐ Design a way to track the response of your mailer, so you can keep track of results.

☐ Research the opportunities involved in database or relationship marketing. See the Glossary for a definition.

☐ Observe how your future competitors operate.

Do their media mixes seem effective? How do they advertise?

What can you learn from their strategies?

☐ Explore the option of using an advertising agency for assistance in developing an overall advertising campaign.

Can an advertising agency save you time and money because of its expertise and connections?

Is a particular agency more reputable and comparable in cost to other advertising agencies?

☐ Review industry publications and pick out ads that catch your eye. Be aware of what makes a good ad and keep examples of them in a file for future reference.

☐ Look for competitor ads in local, regional, or national newspapers and magazines. Keep a file on these ads too.

☐ Introduce yourself to a local printer to get suggestions on where to learn more about the printing business.

   ☐ Find out what type of printer you will most likely need; for example, quick printing, light commercial printing, web press printing, or large commercial printing.

   ☐ Investigate how prices are determined.

   ☐ Familiarize yourself with common printing terms such as bleeds, screens, halftones, special effects, and quantities.

   ☐ Ask about how to get print bids for advertising literature and ads.

Sales Strategies

A sales team often carries out many of the marketing strategies a company develops for itself. Salespeople communicate with a market through a variety of marketing communications methods, such as telemarketing, in-person sales presentations, and direct mail. If you decide to have a sales team in your new venture, which sales methods your team will use depends on your general sales department's goals and your type of business. Even if you don't plan on having a sales team on staff when you open your doors, quickly review the checklists that follow so you can be better informed and knowledgeable about what you'll need to think through and decide on once you realize a sales department will be necessary for your business to remain competitive and successful. Don't make the wrong move when it comes to knowing all your sales strategy options!

General Sales Department Goals Checklist

To ensure clearer communications between your sales staff and other departments, develop general department goals that will help streamline in-house operations and satisfy your customers. Consider these options.

☐ Define the role of sales in your marketing strategy.

Will you need a sales team to begin your operations, or do you anticipate the need for a sales team later on?

What sales strategies can your sales team use to help carry out your overall marketing communications strategy?

Will you rely on media to increase sales or will you do in-person sales calls?

☐ Consider your sales staffing options:

    ☐ An in-house staff.

    ☐ Representative firms — see the Glossary for definition.

    ☐ Direct sales — no sales staff necessary because mail piece or advertisement becomes salesperson.

    ☐ Do-it-yourself.

☐ If an in-house staff is desired, you'll need to set up a process to:

    ☐ Recruit, select, and hire qualified team players.

    ☐ Educate them on your product or service.

    ☐ Train them on how to sell your product or service.

    ☐ Determine sales territories, if necessary.

    ☐ Develop compensation programs for the sales team.

    ☐ Motivate, evaluate, and measure performance.

☐ Identify key customer accounts and develop sales strategies that will help close a sale quickly and efficiently.

☐ Determine how often you will meet with your sales team, and develop a schedule of regular meetings to ask your salespeople for customer feedback and data. Let them know about:

    ☐ Upcoming advertising campaigns, such as a direct mail piece or an ad in a local newspaper.

    ☐ Any existing problems in production or manufacturing that will affect product deadlines and promised delivery dates.

    ☐ Increases or decreases in the cost of any of your products or services, including temporary discount offers or permanent increases.

    ☐ Accounting problems with a particular customer.

Direct Sales Strategies Checklist

Playing the business game means getting out and meeting with the players one on one. As a result, one of the most common ways a business communicates with its prospective customers is through direct sales.

☐ Ensure you and your sales team are always very professional in appearance. Be well-groomed and appropriately dressed.

☐ Choose how you'll make your sales calls.

    ☐ By telephone (telemarketing)

    ☐ Direct mail piece

    ☐ In-person

    ☐ Video

☐ Examine and refine your sales presentation.

> How will you greet or introduce yourself to prospects?
>
> How do you want to present or inform the prospect about your product or service?

☐ Create a friendly, professional sales environment for your customers, whether it's a retail store, your home or business office, or a third-party setting, such as a restaurant.

☐ Develop a policy on customer service.

> Will you take the extra steps necessary to help someone, even though it's clear she'll not purchase from you immediately?
>
> Will you give free how-to advice if it means possibly losing a sale or opportunity to perform your service at that time?
>
> What kind of return policy will you offer?
>
> Will you or your employees refer customers to competitors, if you do not have what the customer needs?

☐ Develop an effective, follow-up system for customer inquiries that'll help ensure customer satisfaction and inspire referrals.

    ☐ Create informational sales literature on each of your products or services so you have some material on hand when needed.

    ☐ Keep track of who makes inquiries and make sure you develop a process that ensures follow up within 48 hours of an inquiry.

Marketing Plans

Writing a marketing plan is much like writing a game plan for a particular sport. The business owner and sports coach alike are both detailing goals, procedures, and methods that'll help them achieve their ultimate goal of winning the game!

By writing down the specifics of a marketing plan, you can clearly indicate how to accomplish your company's marketing goals. Even though this make take some discipline on your part, if you bite the bullet here and consider these checklists' activities, you'll learn what to research and how to organize your findings into a readable, useful marketing plan.

Marketing Plan Components Checklist

How long or short your marketing plan will be depends on the scope of your research and the amount of detail you want to include in your plan. Regardless of length, your marketing plan should contain most, if not all, of the information mentioned in this checklist.

☐ Write an introduction for your marketing plan.

What's your purpose behind writing the plan?

What products or services are you selling?

What states do you sell your products or services in?

☐ Include a section on your product or service.

   ☐ Specify where it's used, how it's used, and why it's needed.

☐ List your specific goals and objectives for your new business.

☐ Do an external evaluation of your marketplace. Include:

   ☐ Any assumptions about the marketplace you're making that could affect your goals and objectives;

   ☐ The size and type of your market; and

   ☐ The strengths and weaknesses of your competitors.

☐ Do an internal evaluation of your marketplace. Include:

   ☐ A sales forecast of the first three years of business;

   ☐ A list of your company's strengths and weaknesses in the market;

   ☐ An analysis of how you're positioned in the market; and

   ☐ An analysis of how you expect to do financially in the first years of operation.

☐ Discuss your overall marketing strategy for your business. Consider:

What needs to happen before any of your sales forecasts become a reality?

What are the changing and current trends in your marketplace?

How do you propose to reach your customers? What's your media mix and how much sales revenue is needed to break even on your advertising?

☐ Prepare a financial summary to help you see if your marketing strategy and plan will work at a profit.

   ☐ Try to cover gross margins, sales and marketing expenses, investment requirements, and returns on investments.

   ☐ Have your accountant review your predictions and provide advice on layout and figures.

Marketing Budgets

You probably wouldn't consider financing a new car or computer without first looking at your income and expenses to see if such a purchase was affordable. Likewise, you don't want to buy advertising time, create sales literature, or hire a complete staff of salespeople without first researching your business' potential sales figures and anticipated marketing expenses.

Because many new start-ups have a limited amount of capital and funding, most new business owners use their own money for advertising and marketing budgets. As a result, many such budgets are often small to start off with, but they usually increase as effective strategies are employed and sales begin to increase.

Take the time to review the checklists in this section so you're more familiar with the marketing budget process. See if you can come up with a marketing budget based on your own forecasting and budgeting experience.

Budgeting Basics Checklist

Regardless of whether or not you'll have an accountant do your financial statements and bookkeeping, it makes good business sense to, at a minimum, have a basic understanding of the factors that go into budgeting. The checklist featured below includes a couple of budgeting basics you can think about when formulating your marketing budget. Refer to Chapter 2 for more checklists and information regarding financial issues.

☐ Forecast the total sales figure you anticipate for the first year of operation. Consider factors that will most likely increase sales in your first year.

   Will you be increasing your advertising?

   Will you be developing more marketing strategies?

   Will you be hiring salespeople?

☐ Calculate the costs you anticipate for the implementation of your marketing strategies.

   ☐ Review trade and professional publications for information on average business expenses in your industry.

   ☐ Ask other business owners how they operate, the costs involved, and any advice they can give on budgeting for marketing expenses.

   ☐ Study your competitors' advertising expenditures.

 Because you're starting a new business, you'll have to anticipate spending a lot of time and money educating your market about your product or service through advertising and public relations.

☐ Look hard for any and all data to help you budget your marketing dollars.

☐ Study target markets and media options to determine where to best spend your marketing dollars.

Strategies and Tips

Nearly all new businesses will have to rely on a good marketing strategy to succeed in their marketplaces. If you've completed checking off the applicable activities listed in this chapter's checklists, you're doing well in achieving this goal. Review these extra tips and sources to augment your initial marketing plan of action.

- The first part of any public relations plan is to assess the market. In developing a web site, this means surfing different web sites to see what's out there. Check out the competition and collect good and bad web site examples for reference and models.

- According to a 1995 study by Netsmart, 81 percent of users turn to the Internet to research new products or services. (This type of figure gives PR and marketing pros heart palpitations!)

- Use testimonials from existing customers to encourage more sales and provide more credibility.

- Consider what trade shows may benefit your business and plan on attending.

- Network with related or complementary businesses to refer customers back and forth.

- Your goal is to buy media advertising that reaches the most qualified prospects for the lowest cost.

- At all costs, be professional in your advertising. Make sure your printed ads are error free, well-balanced, and visually pleasing.

- Companies that are new to the marketplace will ordinarily have to spend more for advertising than their established counterparts.

- Studies show that most sales are made after nine advertising exposures to a product or service, and only every third media exposure gets seen by prospects.

Helpful Resources

Here are some solid marketing resources to consider. For more of the same, you can refer to the appendices in the back of the book for info on SBDCs, biz magazines and other publications, and online resources for small business.

American Marketing Association (AMA)
(312) 831-2780

A national association that promotes education and professional development in the marketing field. Publishes *Marketing News*.

A Business Guide to the Federal Trade Commission's Mail Order Rule
Federal Trade Commission
(202) 326-2222

If you're into mail order, this free publication on the FTC's Mail Order Rule is a must.

Guerrilla Marketing
Houghton Mifflin Company
(800) 225-3362

A classic on ways to promote and market your biz on a budget, but with punch.

How to Develop Successful Sales Promotions
American Management Association
1 (888) 281-5092

Minimize your sales promotion risks and maximize your chances of success by applying the knowledge, techniques, and skills in this course book.

Looking Good in Print
Ventana Communications
(919) 544-9404

Presents tips, techniques, and guidance on producing attractive and effective newsletters, advertisements, brochures, and other communication pieces.

Marketing for Small Business: An Overview
U.S. Small Business Administration
(800) 872-5627

Worth the couple of bucks for its extensive bibliography and basic overview of effective marketing strategies.

Marketing Research Association
(860) 257-4008

Publishes several resources on research services, data collection, and promoting marketing and opinion research to consumers.

National Trade and Professional Association Directory
Columbia Books
(202) 898-0662

You'll find a gold mine of secondary research and mailing list info here. Check out an edition at the local library or call the publisher.

Start Up Marketing
Career Press
(800) 227-3371

Get the results you want for your start-up with a small budget.

U.S. Department of Commerce
(202) 482-2000

You can request a list of free publications on economic development from this department. Several discuss marketing aspects and topics.

Helpful Resources from The Oasis Press

The Oasis Press — The Leading Publisher of Small Business Information also has a collection of valuable marketing resources that can be of assistance. You can order these books from your local bookstore, or call the company directly at:

The Oasis Press
(800) 228-2275

Advertising Without an Agency: A Comprehensive Guide

Take the guesswork out of advertising decisions for your small business with this comprehensive guide.

Connecting Online: Creating a Successful Image on the Internet

A cutting-edge book on a new aspect of public relations — the company web site. Learn about the Internet and how to market yourself there.

Customer Engineering: Cutting Edge Selling Strategies

A great resource for helping you research your customers, develop a database, and generate sales leads.

Developing International Markets: Secrets of Funding and Exploiting Prospects

This book's practical, real-life info and examples will get you on the high road to international marketplaces.

Friendship Marketing: Growing Your Business by Cultivating Strategic Relationships

Shows how building relationships is the key to business development and personal fulfillment. Learn how to be a friend, listen, build a team, and do strategic planning.

Keeping Score: An Inside Look At Sports Marketing

If your biz would benefit from marketing through the multi-billion dollar sports industry, check this book out. It's a start-to-finish guide for playing ball in the big leagues.

Know Your Market: How to Do Low-Cost Market Research

Find out where to go and how to get the market research info you need with this do-it-yourself guide.

Mail Order Legal Guide

An all-in-one look at how to market your biz through the mail. Covers the do's and don'ts from the FTC and state legal requirements.

Marketing for the New Millennium

One step above the usual how-to marketing books, this forward-looking book discusses combining marketing techniques and angles for the Year 2000 and beyond.

Marketing Mastery: Your Seven Step Guide to Success

Get your product or service off the ground and running with this beginner's look and trek through marketing.

Navigating the Marketplace: Growth Strategies for Your Business

Design your biz to target different types of customers and learn to recognize solid marketing strategies and techniques to make sure you get the most out of your marketing efforts.

Power Marketing for Small Business

A great marketing resource for the start-up biz owner — a friendly, basic look at the world of marketing and advertising.

Prospecting for Gold: 101 Ways to Market Yourself and Strike Gold in Sales

Jumpstart your sales planning with workable ideas on marketing products or services and prospecting for new sales sources.

Public Relations Marketing: Making a Splash Without Much Cash

Get this book and learn how to make your own publicity opportunities for very little cost! This is a terrific source for getting your biz's PR program in full swing, without striking out!

Secrets to High Ticket Selling

Written by a GM sales standout, you'll learn negotiating skills, language patterns, and subtle gestures that inspire buyers, and ways to close the sale so both parties are smiling. Good reading for you and your sales staff.

Selling Services: Marketing for the Consulting Professional

Make the right decisions to hook new clients and close the sale. Anyone with a service business will benefit from this book's tip-top marketing strategies.

Successful Network Marketing for the 21st Century

A book for those interested in network marketing — get the hard facts about starting a biz with multi-leveled marketing structures and more.

TargetSmart: Database Marketing for the Small Business

Database marketing is a hot commodity for both big and small biz. Don't miss out on learning more about this potential marketing strategy.

The Twenty-One Sales in a Sale: What Sales Are You Missing?

Discover what's lacking from your sales technique by understanding every single step of a successful sales presentation. This could be a good training resource for any in-house sales staff you may hire.

Web Wise: A Simplified Management Guide for the Development of a Successful Web Site

Manage the design, maintenance, and hosting of your web site with the skill and savvy of a web expert. This book weaves a strong strategy for being "web wise" and managing a stellar site.

Notes

Plan of Action for Marketing Strategies

Your company will market products or services as a:
☐ Retailer   ☐ Wholesaler   ☐ Manufacturer   ☐ Service company

Use this planning tool to organize and prioritize the activities in this chapter that you've checked off. Don't feel you have to list all the activities you have checked off. Simply start with the top ten most important ones and go from there, or do whatever is easiest for you. Make plenty of copies of this cut-out worksheet for your planning and organizing activities for this chapter.

Action to be Taken	Begin Date	Who	Deadline

Plan of Action (continued)

Action to be Taken	Begin Date	Who	Deadline

Chapter 4

If Your Business Will Have Employees

Introduction

Many new start-ups begin as one-person operations, but as sales increase and the businesses grow, they must look to others to share in the workload.

When you hire employees, the business game rule book thickens. In particular, a slew of federal regulations will mandate and affect your actions and communications with your future employees. From guidelines on what you can and cannot ask during an employee interview to regulations for on-the-job safety, you'll need to comply with both state and federal employer laws. Keep in mind these regulations are a part of the government's effort to ensure equality and fairness in employee hiring and working conditions; they're not an attempt to control you or your business, even though you may feel that way at times.

Even if you'll be hiring just one employee, you'll need to know the areas outlined in this chapter's checklists, which help you recognize the initial processes for staffing your business; the laws and filings you'll need to understand before you hire your employees; and some of the personnel paperwork you should anticipate.

Remember you're not considered an employee of your sole proprietorship or partnership. Anyone else working for your business — with the possible exception of your spouse or child — will be considered an employee. The requirements outlined in this chapter are for any type of business, regardless of its legal form or whether it's a retail, manufacturing, wholesale, service, or construction company.

First Aid for Hiring Employees

People Investment: Making Your Hiring Decisions Pay Off for Everyone and *SmartStart Your (State) Business* are two good resources for dealing with the legal considerations and potential paperwork of being an employer. For more information on these resources, contact the publisher at the toll-free number listed below.

People Investment
SmartStart Your (State) Business
The Oasis Press
(800) 228-2275

In addition, you will find a number of other helpful resources located at the end of this chapter. Ranging from helpful government agencies to various publications, the Helpful Resources section will make being the captain of your own team easier.

Staffing Your Business

Assuming you won't have an outside employment agency do the recruiting and hiring of your employees, you'll have to organize a thorough, well-thought-out hiring procedure to staff your own business. This staffing procedure will take you from the creation of job descriptions to the orientation and training of the individuals you hire.

By taking the time to evaluate the hiring processes now, you'll be better prepared personally and financially once you begin to hire employees. You'll also reduce confusion and misunderstandings because of this initial preplanning. By completing the activities featured in the checklists for this section, you'll have a solid beginning for an in-house hiring and staffing procedure.

Initial Definitions Checklist

The first step for any future employer is to recruit and hire qualified individuals for specific, well-defined job positions. To accomplish this primary goal, first write down some initial position definitions and goals. Follow the steps below to help ensure a successful staffing procedure.

☐ List all the job positions you'll need to fill before opening your doors. Your descriptions should include items, such as:

    ☐ Job titles;

☐ Job duties; for example, describe the everyday activities and functions of the position;

☐ Job requirements; for example, descriptions of the necessary tasks and the necessary tools and equipment for a particular job;

☐ Employee qualifications; for example, past experience, education, and special licenses;

☐ Wage and salary information; for example, determine what is considered a fair wage or salary for a particular job position by conducting an informal survey of other businesses or colleagues; and

☐ Benefits; for example, medical insurance, holiday pay, sick leave, and retirement plans.

Recruiting and Selecting Checklist

Finding the right person for any job within your new start-up is crucial because you want to ensure your employees are competent, professional, and enthusiastic about their new positions so your prospective customers feel confident and satisfied about their relationship with your new business. To find these qualified individuals, review the checklist below.

☐ Prepare application forms.

    ☐ Create a separate consent form that allows you to contact an applicant's previous employers.

    ☐ Ensure you don't violate anti-discrimination laws when developing personnel questionnaires and application forms. Only ask questions related to skills needed to perform the job.

☐ Determine how you'll advertise available positions.

    ☐ Informal recruiting, such as through business associates, friends, and community resources;

    ☐ Newspaper ads;

    ☐ Magazine ads;

    ☐ Through private employment agencies;

    ☐ Through state employment services; or

    ☐ Through university or community college campus career centers.

☐ Sift through all returned application forms and compare how each applicant measures up to the job requirements.

☐ Let each applicant know you've received his application and the status of the selection process.

☐ Screen out those applicants that don't meet your minimum job qualifications.

☐ Rank the remaining applications in the priority of best qualified first and then downwards from there.

☐ Contact those applicants who are going to be interviewed for the position.

☐ Determine if you'll conduct informal or formal interviews.

☐ Prepare all your questions beforehand.

☐ Comply with state and federal anti-discrimination laws when asking interview questions. Avoid questions pertaining to:

    ☐ Dates of educational background

    ☐ Age, race, or color

    ☐ Sexual preference

    ☐ Marital status

    ☐ Religion

    ☐ Credit status

    ☐ Medical background, health, disability, or physical condition

    ☐ Child care responsibilities

☐ Interview your top five to ten candidates for the position.

☐ Make notes immediately after each interview to remember important comments and thoughts regarding each applicant.

☐ Review your notes, carefully evaluating both the good and bad points of the interview session.

☐ Do a reference check of any applicant you're considering hiring.

    ☐ Check with your state's labor department to obtain guidance on what pre-employment information you can legally request from previous employers or personal references.

☐ If necessary or desired, learn how to legally and properly test the abilities and skills (which are necessary for doing the job) of your final applicants.

☐ Present the job offer to your top candidate.

    ☐ Be clear about what is negotiable and what is not to avoid misunderstandings.

    ☐ Clarify conditions of employment.

- [ ] Obtain a final answer from your top candidate before contacting your other final applicants.

- [ ] If yes, then notify all other final applicants the position has been filled.

Training and Orientation Checklist

After you've hired your new employees, you're ready to train and orient them so their transition into your business is as smooth and as comfortable as possible. Taking the time now to formulate training and orientation strategies will only make this task easier once you have employees. Review this checklist to help you create a basic training and orientation procedure.

- [ ] Have the new employee fill in necessary paperwork. See the Personnel Recordkeeping Checklist later in this chapter.

- [ ] Take the new employee on a tour of the business' facilities.

  - [ ] Introduce employees to one another.
  - [ ] Explain overall operations so the new employee gets the big picture.
  - [ ] Point out break areas, restrooms, or nearby locations for lunch breaks.
  - [ ] Provide an informal history of the business.

- [ ] Provide the employee with an employee handbook.

- [ ] Explain the purpose and function of the employee's workstation.

- [ ] Describe the chain of command, work relationships, and who the employee should go to with questions about the job.

- [ ] Briefly explain the relationship of the employee's department to other departments.

- [ ] Review the new employee's particular job.

- [ ] Ensure that the employee knows who her immediate supervisor is.

- [ ] Briefly explain the purpose of the job.

- [ ] Briefly explain the training; how long it'll last and what's involved.

- [ ] Develop an initial training process for the new employee.

  - [ ] Decide who'll train the employee.
  - [ ] Determine the length of time of the training.
  - [ ] Figure the costs involved in the training; for example, the wages of the trainer or the tuition for specialized classroom training.
  - [ ] Evaluate the training process to track progress and productivity.

☐ In addition to the above initial employee training procedure, consider developing a training program to address:

  ☐ Companywide needs, such as workplace safety, use of equipment, or employee understanding of the benefits and attributes of each product or service.

  ☐ Individual employee needs, such as career advancement through in-house promotion, personal and professional growth through continued education, or professional challenges through change in responsibility or workload.

Other Staffing Options Checklist

If you don't think you'll need to hire full-time, permanent help when starting your new business, but you do anticipate the need for some extra help occasionally, then explore the staffing options listed below. These options can save you a significant amount of time and money, especially when dealing with employer-related paperwork and payroll taxes.

These options, however, must be carefully investigated so you don't unknowingly treat an individual as an employee for tax purposes. Definitions of these options are listed in the Glossary.

☐ Use temporary employees from an established temporary employment agency.

> Are there any temporary employment agencies in your area you could call to get more information on how their operations work?
>
> Is the temp agency licensed by the state?
>
> What types of temps does the agency have available?
>
> How do you go about contracting services with the temp agency?

☐ Farm out work to independent contractors.

  ☐ Contact the Internal Revenue Service (IRS) for its definition and qualifications regarding independent contractors versus employees for tax treatment purposes.

  ☐ Contact your state tax and labor departments for any guidelines on how they view independent contractors versus employees.

☐ Consider leasing employees through an established leasing company.

  ☐ Contact the state controller's office or attorney general to find out what controls, if any, the state has over employee leasing services.

Miscellaneous Staffing Activities Checklist

The activities below are some to consider completing before hiring employees. By taking a look at some of these issues at this time, you'll streamline your personnel procedures and goals for the future and make a positive first impression on your new staff.

In addition, each of these activities should be a part of your company policy manual and employee handbook. Your findings here can be easily included in your manual and handbook. Refer to the the Company Policy Manual Checklist for more information.

☐ Develop a voluntary affirmative action program. See the Glossary for a definition.

    ☐ Contact your local Equal Employment Opportunity Commission (EEOC) office for information on how to do this.

☐ Forecast initial and long-term staffing requirements.

In what areas do you need the most employees to start-up?
What departments or positions do you see as growing the quickest?
How many additional sales will be needed to support the hiring of new employees?

☐ Develop a salary schedule.

What will be the starting and highest wages or salaries for each position in your business?
By what criteria will increases in wages or salaries be awarded? Strictly by job performance, by length of service, or by supervisor recommendation? Or what about a combination of these qualifiers?
How will your business pay or adjust for these increases in wages or salaries?

☐ Prepare and develop an employee evaluation system. Consider:

How will you evaluate employee job performance?
Who will be responsible for reviewing employees?
How often will you do employee reviews?

☐ Decide if your business will be able to offer an employee retirement plan. If it will, you will need to:

    ☐ Comply with the Employee Retirement Income Security Act of 1974 (ERISA).

    ☐ Enlist the help of an attorney to coordinate your responsibilities under ERISA.

☐ Determine discretionary benefits, such as how your company will deal with paid vacation, sick pay, parental leave, educational assistance, and child care — to name a few.

☐ Develop procedures for promoting and terminating employees.

☐ Determine how you will deal with reducing your staff, if the situation should warrant it.

☐ Evaluate advantages and disadvantages of allowing flexible work schedules for employees.

 How important is it in terms of serving the clients to have a flexible work schedule?

How does a flexible work schedule, if desired, affect the communications and coordination of work or tasks among staff members?

What are the additional financial costs of having a flexible work schedule?

What is the effect of a flexible work schedule on your ability to supervise and evaluate the performance of staff members?

Government Regulations and Taxes for Employers

Not only does the government have rules and regulations about hiring and staffing procedures, such as equal opportunity and anti-discrimination laws, it also has a myriad of laws that specifically cover the employer-employee relationship. The checklists in this section attempt to cover the laws, registrations, filings, and taxes you must deal with once you hire your first employee. Take care to review these items very carefully. The business game can get a little complicated at this point.

Whenever possible throughout this section, the government agency that handles a particular regulation or requirement is listed in parentheses, or mentioned in the checklist activity itself, so you have an idea of where to go for more information and details. Most of these agencies' addresses and phone numbers are listed in the Helpful Resources section at the end of this chapter.

You'll find two comprehensive checklists in this section: one on federal regulations and taxes and the other on state and local regulations and taxes.

Federal Employer Regulations and Taxes Checklist

This checklist includes the U.S. government's laws and acts that cover employees. Some of the acts and laws may or may not apply to your business; however, it's your responsibility to determine which ones will and won't apply. This checklist is a good starting point.

- ☐ Apply for a federal employer identification number (EIN) by requesting *Form SS-4, Application for Employer Identification Number.* (Your local IRS office)

- ☐ Research the requirements outlined in the Americans with Disabilities Act of 1990 (ADA). (Your local EEOC office or the U.S. Department of Justice in Washington, D.C.)

- ☐ Learn about the federal Family and Medical Leave Act of 1993 to see if your new business is covered under its qualifiers. (U.S. Department of Labor)

- ☐ Comply with ERISA requirements if offering employees fringe benefits, such as pension plans, welfare plan benefits, or profit-sharing plans. (IRS or the U.S. Department of Labor)

- ☐ Know how the federal requirements of the Occupational Safety and Health Act of 1970 (OSHA) will affect your workplace safety procedures and programs.

  - ☐ Contact your local federal OSHA office (or state equivalent) and request a free consultation of what OSHA standards your business needs to be aware of before opening its doors. Some basic federal OSHA requirements include:

    - ☐ Posting a permanent notice to employees regarding job safety in the workplace.

    - ☐ Keeping a log of all job-related injuries and illnesses on federal *Form 200.*

- ☐ Obtain a copy of the Fair Labor and Standards Act (FLSA) from the U.S. Department of Labor and review the federal requirements for:

  - ☐ Child labor laws

  - ☐ Minimum wage

  - ☐ Overtime pay

  - ☐ Rest periods and meal breaks

☐ Familiarize yourself with the following federal anti-discrimination laws by contacting the EEOC office nearest you. Only a few of these laws may apply to you as a start-up, but learn about them for possible future application:

    ☐ Title VII of the Civil Rights Act of 1964

    ☐ Pregnancy Discrimination Act

    ☐ Executive Order 11246

    ☐ Equal Pay Act of 1963

    ☐ Age Discrimination in Employment Act of 1967

    ☐ Rehabilitation Act of 1973

    ☐ Vietnam-Era Veteran Readjustment Assistance Act of 1974

    ☐ Veterans Reemployment Rights Act of 1994

☐ Learn about your potential liability for sexual harassment in the workplace.

What is sexual harassment?

What types of harassment are there, and how has the EEOC dealt with them in the past?

☐ Obtain a copy of the Immigration Reform and Control Act of 1986 (IRCA). (U.S. Immigration and Naturalization Service – INS)

☐ Get several copies of *Form I-9, Employment Eligibility Verification*, from the INS.

    ☐ Be sure all your employees fill out this form; it's a federal requirement.

    ☐ Make a separate personnel file for I-9 forms. You don't want to file I-9 forms with regular personnel files because the federal government can demand to see I-9 forms at any time, and you don't want them to have access to your other personnel paperwork as well.

☐ Be prepared to withhold the following federal taxes from your employee's wages:

    ☐ Income tax

    ☐ Social Security (FICA) tax

☐ As an employer, you'll be required to pay:

    ☐ Social Security (FICA) tax; and

    ☐ Federal unemployment tax (FUTA), if you pay wages of more than $1,500 or more during a calendar year or if one or more employees work at least a portion of the day during 20 different calendar weeks during the year.

☐ Be prepared to furnish all new employees with *Form W-4, Withholding Allowance Certificate*.

    ☐ Get copies of *Form W-4* from your local IRS office.

    ☐ Have each employee complete and return *Form W-4* to you.

    ☐ At the end of each year, furnish each employee with copies of *Form W-2, Annual Wage and Tax Statement*, showing taxable wages paid during the preceding calendar year and the tax withheld.

☐ Note: for any independent contractor you employ during a calendar year, and to whom you pay more than $600 to in compensation, you must file *Form 1099-MISC* with the IRS.

State (and Local) Employer Regulations and Taxes Checklist

State and local governments have their own sets of employer laws and taxes. Your best bet for knowing your state-specific employer laws is to contact your state's economic development department or one-stop business center and request a business kit of information for start-up employers. You could also contact the various agencies within the appropriate labor department in your state.

Local employer requirements can be researched through your local city hall or county clerk's office. Use the checklist below as a guide in your state-specific research.

☐ Register as an employer with the appropriate state agencies, for example, the employment division and the revenue department.

☐ Research any state-mandated family leave law that may apply to your business. (Many states have family leave laws that cover employers not covered by the federal law.)

☐ See if your state requires a workers' compensation insurance for employees — nearly all states do — and investigate how to go about obtaining this insurance.

    Is there a state-run workers' compensation insurance carrier?

    How much will this insurance cost you? For example, will you be able to join a group policy that offers reduced rates and premiums?

    How can you reduce this insurance cost?

☐ Request information from your state's occupational safety and health department and see if you need to:

- [ ] Make any filings or reports with them;

- [ ] Display any state safety posters;

- [ ] Comply with any safety standards beyond those required by federal OSHA;

- [ ] Take advantage of any free, on-site consultative programs that might be available for state employers; and

- [ ] Complete a written safety program and create a safety committee, if required.

- [ ] Investigate state wage-hour laws to see if any go beyond what's required of federal FLSA requirements. Don't forget to check on:

  - [ ] Child labor laws;

  - [ ] Minimum wage requirements and how they apply to covered employees, student workers, and disabled workers;

  - [ ] Overtime pay;

  - [ ] Pay period minimums;

  - [ ] Rest periods and meal breaks; and

  - [ ] Right-to-work laws.

- [ ] Compare state anti-discrimination laws with federal anti-discrimination laws to pinpoint any major differences.

- [ ] Withhold these state taxes from your employee's wages, if applicable:

  - [ ] Income tax

  - [ ] State disability insurance

- [ ] As an employer, you may be required to pay a state unemployment tax or workers' compensation insurance tax.

  - [ ] Contact your state labor department or economic development department for more specifics on rates and other potential employer taxes.

- [ ] Research how to make employer tax payments and to which departments.

  What forms will you need?
  What is the payment schedule or deadline?
  How do you figure the taxes?

- [ ] Determine how independent contractor payments are recorded and filed for your state.

☐ Contact all labor-related state agencies to ensure you have all the required posters for issues regarding minimum wage, child labor, overtime, unemployment benefits, and others.

☐ Contact your county clerk's office to research any applicable employer requirements for local government.

☐ Check with your local fire department to ensure you comply with fire code and safety standards for your workplace.

Personnel Paperwork

As you can imagine, all the paperwork generated by hiring employees and ensuring compliance with the numerous employer regulations can add up quickly. If you don't have a system for organizing all of these materials, you could find yourself in an office management nightmare, not knowing when you hired someone, when that person quit, or if she received the required *Form W-2* at the end of the calendar year. In addition, if you fail to keep accurate records on such things as tax payments, required filings, and OSHA procedures, you could be setting yourself up for some hefty penalties. You need to ensure your personnel files are organized and maintained efficiently.

Besides maintaining your personnel files, another form of initial paperwork is the development of your company's personnel policy manual. The minute you hire new employees, you need to clarify for them, in writing, the policies they'll need and want to know about before starting their first day on the job, such as business hours, paid vacation, sick pay, pay periods, and fringe benefits. Many other policies need to be clarified as well, such as smoking rules, employee safety, performance review, dress code, and sexual harassment.

Depending on your type of business, your policies can vary in number and specifics. Developing a company policy manual before hiring your first employee will help ensure clearer communications with your staff, provide a framework for consistency and fairness, and provide written guidelines for human resource decisions. Preventing personnel problems before they occur is important to smooth business operations and doing so usually saves time and money in the long run.

Review the checklists in this section for an overview of personnel recordkeeping and company policy manuals.

Personnel Recordkeeping Checklist

Without strong recordkeeping procedures, you don't have a convenient, quick-read history of your team players or what activities you have or have not done on their behalf. You also won't have the information required by the government. Review the checklist below so you have a better idea of your recordkeeping requirements.

☐ Ensure each employee's personnel file includes the following:

   ☐ A completed company application form;

   ☐ A copy of the job description;

   ☐ Additional application materials, such as letters of reference or college transcripts;

   ☐ Emergency contact information;

   ☐ Pre-employment job-related test results, if given;

   ☐ Selection findings, if formalized;

   ☐ Employment contract or agreement, if used;

   ☐ A completed *Form W-4*;

   ☐ Any required state taxation forms;

   ☐ Payroll authorization form;

   ☐ Federal unemployment tax (FUTA) information;

   ☐ Records of wages and taxes;

   ☐ Records of hours worked;

   ☐ Records of employment history with the company; and

   ☐ Records of performance.

☐ Keep any medical records separate from personnel files.

   ☐ Know the laws pertaining to what you can and cannot have in the medical files.

Company Policy Manual Checklist

A company policy manual is your first step toward establishing written guidelines for employer-employee communications. From your policy manual, you can write your employee handbook. See the Glossary for the definitions of each. *A Company Policy & Personnel Workbook* is particularly helpful for the new start-up creating and developing its first manual.

Review the checklist below to get an idea of a policy manual outline and what to do to ensure accuracy and efficiency.

☐ As a general outline, have your company policy manual contain the following information:

  ☐ Benefits

  ☐ Career opportunities

  ☐ Company background

  ☐ Employee evaluation procedures

  ☐ Employee grievance procedures

  ☐ Employee rules and regulations

  ☐ Employee safety

  ☐ Employee/management relations

  ☐ General policies and procedures

  ☐ Pay rates and schedules

☐ Explain the company's policy on smoking, sexual harassment, and employee privacy.

☐ Have your attorney review your policy manual to ensure accuracy with all applicable business and employer laws.

☐ Establish a review and updating procedure for the manual.

☐ Create an employee handbook from your company policy manual, if desired.

Strategies and Tips

Hiring employees is always a big undertaking, but it's also a very exciting one. By hiring employees you're adding a whole new dimension to your business. This is your team. Do your best to recruit and hire the most qualified people for the jobs, play by the rules set forth by the various government agencies, and keep your paperwork in order. If you do all of this, the business game will not be as intimidating. Here are some strategies and tips to help build and maintain a sound and satisfied business team.

- The skills and attitudes of your future employees will help build your business' credibility and reputation and those of its products or services. Look hard and long for the right members of your business team; it can make a difference in whether you win or lose in the business game.

- Medical exams cannot be used as a screening device for hiring employees. If you want to include medical exams in your hiring process, contact your workers' compensation department, as well as a professional adviser on the rules outlined in the Americans with Disabilities Act (ADA).

- The better prepared employees are to assume job positions, the less likely they are to feel out of place and look for employment elsewhere. Orientation provides an employee with information on company benefits or what benefit choices the employee has.

- Many state occupational safety and health agencies offer free, confidential, on-site consultation services for employers who want to ensure they are in compliance with all state and federal OSHA laws. Call your state department of labor to see if your state offers this valuable, helpful service.

- The unemployment tax is one tax you can help reduce on your own. By not overhiring and causing excessive layoffs, by keeping detailed records of why an employee was fired, and by challenging unfounded unemployment claims brought against your business, you will most likely reduce your tax experience rating and save yourself some money.

- Many of the state employment agencies offer free employer handbooks that explain the unemployment taxing and benefit procedures for their respective states. It would be worth a phone call to get this handbook before you hire employees.

- A company policy manual is critical in establishing clear communications with your future employees. Make it a priority, before you start hiring, to have your thoughts, procedures, and policies down on paper.

Helpful Resources

Here are some good employer resources to consider. For more of the same, you can refer to the appendices in the back of the book for info on SBDCs, biz magazines and other publications, and online resources for small business.

Circular E, Employer's Tax Guide
Internal Revenue Service
(800) 829-3676

Explains federal income tax withholding and Social Security tax requirements. The good news? It's free!

EEOC Technical Assistance Guide
Equal Employment Opportunity Commission (EEOC)
(800) 669-3362

A free listing of nonprofit resources offering technical assistance related to EEOC regulations, including The Americans with Disabilities Act.

Employer's Handbook
U.S. Immigration and Naturalization Service (INS)
(800) 755-0777

A free publication to help you with INS employment regulations.

Hiring Independent Contractors: The Employer's Legal Guide
Nolo Press
(800) 992-6656

See how you can hire independent contractors and reap the financial rewards while staying out of trouble with the IRS.

How to Comply with Federal Employee Laws
London Publishing
(800) 378-6573

A good reference for the start-up.

Personnel Planning Guide
Dearborn Financial Publishing
(800) 621-9621

Get your personnel books in order with this 1-2-3 planning guide.

Recordkeeping Requirements for Occupational Injuries and Illnesses
U.S. Department of Labor – OSHA
(202) 219-6666

A free publication that details the recordkeeping requirements of federal OSHA.

Social Security Administration
(800) 772-1213

A toll-free number if you have any questions on Social Security.

Helpful Resources from The Oasis Press

The Oasis Press — The Leading Publisher of Small Business Information also has a collection of valuable marketing resources for biz game rookies. See if any strike your fancy. You can order these books from your local bookstore, or call the company directly at:

The Oasis Press
(800) 228-2275

A Company Policy & Personnel Handbook

Get one step ahead of the crowd by creating your own company policy manual before hiring your first employee. Over 80 models policies and 28 ready-to-use personnel forms for your convenience!

CompControl: The Secrets of Reducing Workers' Compensation Costs

Figure out how workers' compensation works and how you can save money and improve worker safety.

Draw the Line: A Sexual Harassment-Free Workplace

Learn about sexual harassment and creating a nonhostile work environment for everyone. Provides a sample harassment policy and advice on what to do if a sexual harassment claim occurs.

Improving Staff Productivity: Great Ideas to Increase Profits

A clear game plan guides you on how to get the most out of your employees, equipment, and buildings; raise employee morale; improve customer service; and track your system's effectiveness.

Managing People: A Practical Guide

Discussions, exercises, and self-tests boost skills in communicating, delegating, motivating, and developing teams. Get with the managing program with this guide.

People Investment: Making Your Hiring Decisions Pay off for Everyone

If you want great employees, learn how to find and keep them, and avoid legal troubles along the way.

SmartStart Your (State) Business series

A unique start-up guide for small business owners because of its one-stop, federal and state-specific info. Find out what your state's employer laws are and how to comply with them.

Truth About Teams: A Facilitator's Survival Guide

When you're the boss, facilitating teamwork will be one of your biggest hurdles. Learn the techniques and exercises for jumping employee hurdles and creating a winning team!

Plan of Action — for Employees

Your company will need employees in the following areas:
☐ Full-time   ☐ Part-time   ☐ Temporary   ☐ Independent contractors

Use this planning tool to organize and prioritize the activities in this chapter that you've checked off. Don't feel you have to list all the activities you've checked off. Simply start with the top ten most important ones and go from there, or do whatever is easiest for you. Make plenty of copies of this cut-out worksheet for your planning and organizing activities for this chapter.

Action to be Taken	Begin Date	Who	Deadline

Plan of Action (continued)

Action to be Taken	Begin Date	Who	Deadline

Chapter 5

Production and Management

Introduction

One of the most vital and dynamic aspects of your business will be the process of producing your product or service — from production, packaging, shipping and handling to understanding inventory control and warehousing. It's how well you handle this whole group of activities that will set your product or service apart from the competition and give you a unique niche in your particular marketplace, whether you're a one-person, home-based business or a multi-employee manufacturer.

Besides knowing about the ins and outs of production, you'll always be challenged with the actual business management of your soon-to-be growing start-up. Having strong leadership skills and being familiar with the basics of good management will help improve your productivity and streamline your organization.

Having your finger on the pulse of both production and management is a crucial role you'll play as business owner. It'll be your responsibility to make sure inventory levels are adequate, employees are trained sufficiently, and financial indicators are monitored regularly.

This chapter has four main sections that cover some general aspects of production, shipping and receiving, inventory control, and business management. The main goal of each of these sections is to prompt you into knowing more about these vital areas of your business.

The numbers and systems of these areas will help you determine cost-of-goods, prices for your products or services, and how much inventory is needed for normal production. In each of the following sections, pay particular attention to the planning questions. They'll be valuable strategies for you to think about when playing the business game.

First Aid for Production and Management

Many of today's general business books cover some aspects of production, warehousing, shipping, and inventory. However, if you're looking for in-depth resources on these subjects, check out *Fundamentals of Inventory Management and Control* and *How to Plan and Manage Warehouse Operations*, which are both available through the American Management Association (AMA). The AMA also features several books on business management which you'd find valuable in your start-up research. You can call the AMA and request a listing of all their course books, audio books, and training programs.

Fundamentals of Inventory Management and Control
How to Plan and Manage Warehouse Operations
American Management Association (AMA)
1 (888) 281-5092

For more detailed descriptions of the above titles and additional books and sources of information regarding production and warehousing, see the Helpful Resources section at the end of this chapter.

Production

Production is the heart of every business. As a result, you should spend a great deal of time determining how you'll produce what you are in business to sell, whether it includes manufacturing a product or delivering a service.

At first, your production will probably be small in relation to what you hope your future production will be. So to begin, try to determine your start-up production needs as thoroughly as possible. By determining your production needs and their costs, you'll have a better basis on which to figure the prices you'll ask for your product or service.

Budget time for determining your product's or service's price. You may even want to consider test marketing your product or service before bringing it out to full-scale production. This means bringing your product or service to your market on a small-scale basis to test its attributes and salability.

You can test market different prices to see which one sells the most; you can test market different packaging methods to see which one receives the best response; or, you can test market different product features or service methods to see which is the most attractive to your target market. Refer to The Oasis Press book, *Power Marketing for Small Business*, for more on test marketing.

No matter what you decide to do to help determine your product's price, packaging, and shipping or your service's price and procedures, you'll be ahead of the game if you take the time to evaluate your production process, needs, and costs. The checklists in this section should inspire you to look at this aspect of your business and be as thorough as possible in your figuring of production costs and setting of production goals.

Determining Your Unit Cost Checklist

Use this checklist to help determine your overall production needs and costs and your cost per product produced or service rendered (unit cost). If needed, find the services of a business consultant with expertise in production to see if you're on the right track.

☐ Establish a list of the production equipment and machinery you'll need to start production of your product or service.

   ☐ Indicate how much each piece of equipment or machinery will cost you for initial start-up and for monthly ongoing use.

_____

_____

_____

_____

_____

_____

_____

☐ List what raw materials you'll need to produce your product or service. Be sure to include every item involved in your production process.

    ☐ Indicate how much each piece of raw material will cost you for initial start-up and for monthly ongoing use.

_____

_____

_____

_____

_____

☐ List any other one-time, start-up production costs you can think of that will influence your initial start-up expenses.

_____

_____

_____

_____

_____

_____

☐ Then list all the ongoing production costs you can think of that'll need to be budgeted for on a monthly basis, including those you listed for production equipment and raw materials. Consider some of the following for your list of ongoing production costs:

    ☐ Figure how many employee hours it will take to produce your product or render your service from start to finish. Be sure to factor their wages and benefits into the ongoing cost.

    ☐ Determine if your product is subject to efficiencies and improvements through machines or better production techniques. If so, what will the ongoing costs be to satisfy this need?

    ☐ Calculate the cost needed to run your company's machinery and equipment, such as power costs, employee wages, maintenance needs, and repair services.

    ☐ Include any ongoing shipping costs and packaging needs.

    ☐ If you'll make service calls in a truck, include your auto expenses on the list.

☐ Include other expenditures, such as rent, taxes, accounting, personnel, and other costs needed to produce the product. (These costs generally cannot be applied directly to a unit, but they must be factored into the cost or you may not be able to make a profit.)

☐ Estimate the number of products to be produced or services to be rendered in a sample, normal production run for one month.

☐ Determine what it'll cost you to produce one product or make one typical service call (a unit cost) by dividing your estimated, average number of products produced or services rendered for one month by the overall estimated ongoing production costs for one month.

☐ Establish a price for your product or service once you know your unit cost.

☐ Estimate your costs for damaged, unacceptable, returned, or unsaleable goods.

Other Production Factors Checklist

Besides knowing your start-up and ongoing production needs and your unit cost, think about some other issues regarding your production process. From issues such as employee safety to shipping and receiving needs, this checklist provides you with some tips on what to think about when evaluating your production process.

☐ Evaluate if you'll be able to produce or provide the quantity of products or services that could be potentially demanded. Think of several different demand levels to see if you can produce the necessary numbers.

What are the impediments to producing more?

Is increasing production important to the success of the business?

Will you be able to maintain the growth? If not, what are the consequences?

☐ Investigate how the businesses and vendors you'll be dealing with in your production process set up and handle the following issues:

☐ Credit policies

☐ Delivery periods and schedules

☐ Discounts

☐ Invoice payment policies

☐ Returns of damaged or defective products

☐ Returns of unused products

- ☐ Returns of unused supplies, materials, or products
- ☐ Shipping charges

☐ Determine if your product will need a bar code. If so:

- ☐ Determine how to reproduce bar codes for your items.
- ☐ Get information about placement, registration, and industry specifications on bar codes from the Uniform Code Council, Inc.

☐ Check with local, state, and federal agencies to see if you will need any approval for selling or producing your product or service.

☐ A testing laboratory, such as Underwriter Laboratories (UL), must certify the safety or quality of your product before you can sell through some channels of distribution.

☐ Determine if you have guarantees from your vendors and suppliers of an acceptable supply of, and set prices on, the inventory items or raw materials needed for production. If not:

Are there alternative sources?

Can you increase your prices without seriously cutting demand?

What can you do to assure your quality meets and remains at a level demanded by your customers?

What can you do to assure yourself the quality of materials or products you purchase from other vendors remains at the level you expect?

☐ If you expand production, consider the changes that will be required.

- ☐ Additional people
- ☐ Additional equipment
- ☐ Additional space
- ☐ Additional money for inventory or raw materials

☐ Check into the cost of waste disposal as a result of production.

Will your production generate waste that's toxic or must be disposed of in a controlled way?

Are there any environmental laws you need to be aware of when planning your production process? See Chapter 6 for more information.

Can you recycle any by-products from your manufacturing or production processes?

☐ Be sure to develop an employee safety awareness program for the procedures and operations in the warehouse.

Will your production require special lighting, venting, or other accommodations to reduce the possibility of industrial accidents or illnesses?

Does your equipment and machinery have all the guards and safety devices they were designed to have?

Do you plan to have a safety training program for truck drivers, forklift operators, and other operators of equipment or machinery?

Do you have on file and available to all users Material Safety Data Sheets regarding each hazardous substance you are using in your operation?

☐ Think about how and where you should incorporate quality control into your production process.

Warehousing and Shipping

To produce a product, you'll need warehousing — you may have a place of your own to warehouse your items, or you may have some other company warehouse them for you. In either case, you must provide a space for your raw materials or inventory items so they're readily available for production and shipping. Finding a suitable warehouse that'll be convenient for you, your future employees, and your future suppliers and shippers is an important step for your production operation to run smoothly and come full circle.

In addition, if you start a mail order business, a manufacturing business, or any other business that requires you to ship to your customers, you'll need to know about the many shipping alternatives and decide which one is best for your business. Besides the popular UPS and Federal Express options, you can ship by rail, air, and water. Keep in mind, in many cases, you can negotiate rates with these shippers. Find out how to qualify for special rates and learn the many different ways to reduce costs in this complex area of business.

Any new businesses will require varying degrees of warehousing and shipping capabilities. Whatever the facilities you're planning, consider the activities listed in this section's checklists to get you thinking about and planning for this very strategic aspect of your production or performance.

Warehousing Planning Checklist

Knowing where to locate your warehouse and how it will be set up and maintained are critical steps for ensuring a smooth order fulfillment operation. Take the time to evaluate your warehousing needs and develop a plan of action.

☐ Determine where you'll warehouse your finished products and the raw materials necessary for production.

> 💡 Will the warehouse be near or adjoining your business office, or will you need to rent warehouse space away from your principal place of doing business?

☐ Evaluate your warehouse location carefully. Check to see if the warehouse building has the following items or features:

  ☐ Easily accessible doors and access for all sizes of trucks that will ship your products or deliver your raw materials;

  ☐ Sufficient electrical wiring for both your present and future needs;

  ☐ Good locations for any signs identifying your company or providing instructions;

  ☐ Enough space for your start-up and future needs; and

  ☐ Adequate fire protection.

☐ Consider how you'll lay out the warehouse so it's efficient and safe for everyone.

> 💡 What types of shelving and storage units will work best in the warehouse?
> How will heavy pallets or packages be handled and stored?
> How will supplies and inventory items be organized?

☐ Develop the required procedures between your sales or order entry department and the warehouse personnel to ensure accurate order fulfillment.

> 💡 What actions will cause an item to be shipped, delivered, or received?
> Who will be responsible for initiating each action?
> How will a purchase order flow through your operations?
> What's the time frame from taking the order to shipping it?

☐ Develop a record of receiving and shipping for your warehouse operations.

☐ Check to see if there are any zoning restrictions regarding your type of business, product, or activity.

☐ If your products are environmentally sensitive or a fire hazard, consider the extra precautions you'll need to implement in your warehousing operations.

> Will you be covered by insurance in case of an accident?
>
> What actions can you take to reduce the possibilities of an accident that would harm the environment?
>
> What type of protective area must you have?
>
> How will you dispose of all waste materials used in production or manufacturing?

Shipment Planning Checklist

Ensuring your shipping and receiving procedure runs smoothly is not only crucial from a production standpoint, it's just as important in terms of customer satisfaction and for building your business' reputation as a reliable source of product or service. Your dependability and promptness in delivering the product or service will go a long way in gaining your customers' satisfaction, referrals, and continued business.

Take the time to review what steps you'll need to take to get your shipping and receiving department in shipshape.

☐ Determine how to ship your product or deliver a service.

☐ Airplane   ☐ Owned truck

☐ Common carrier   ☐ Ship

☐ Leased truck   ☐ Train

☐ Investigate the transportation companies available in your selected means of shipping.

  ☐ Compare rates and services of all the available shipping companies and determine whether it's more of an advantage to use one company over another.

  ☐ Try to negotiate special shipping rates for incoming raw materials or outgoing finished goods.

☐ Choose the person who will be responsible for doing your shipping and receiving.

> Will that person need special training in how to package your product?
>
> What type of skills are necessary for shipping and receiving tasks?

☐ Find out how your shipments or containers need to be labeled.

> Will they need to be specially marked?
>
> What size specifications will you require for your packaging and boxing needs?
>
> If shipping hazardous substances, fragile equipment, or food, what shipping labels or shipping standards must you use or follow?

☐ List what material-handling equipment you'll need for packaging, as well as unloading and loading shipments. For example:

☐ Forklifts   ☐ Racks

☐ Handcarts   ☐ Shrink-wrap equipment and film

☐ Pallets   ☐ Wire cutters

_____

_____

_____

☐ List what shipping supplies and equipment you'll need for start-up.

☐ Boxes   ☐ Scales

☐ Computer/bar code equipment ☐ Shipping labels

☐ Postage meter   ☐ Tape guns, staplers, sealers

_____

_____

_____

☐ Consider developing your own shipping and receiving system by using your own trucks, if feasible.

> What are the advantages and disadvantages of doing this compared to using a common carrier?
>
> How will you schedule your production?

Inventory Control

Most businesses have an inventory of items that are needed for production, as well as an inventory of finished products ready for shipment. Even service businesses often have an inventory of supplies that help them perform their services. Regardless, you're going to want to know how much stock you have on hand, when to reorder supplies, and how much finished product you have available. Consequently, developing an inventory system that will answer these and other crucial questions is a sound business practice.

Inventory control, in conjunction with accounting, will help you get a clearer understanding of the cost of doing business and let you know where your products and supplies are going. For some advice on developing your inventory control system, talk to existing business owners in a line of business similar to yours.

The checklist featured in this section is a brief rundown of some of the things to consider when thinking about how to run your inventory control system.

Inventory Planning Checklist

Keeping tabs on how materials are coming and going from your business is one way to streamline production, but knowing this information takes time and organization. A computer is extremely helpful for completing this activity, and you should really consider purchasing a good inventory program that'll meet the needs of your business.

☐ Decide how you'll keep track of your inventory.

    ☐ Computer program

    ☐ Inventory cards

☐ Determine how you'll monitor the shipping and receiving of finished goods and raw materials.

☐ If you'll have a computer system, consider some of the following questions to see if they apply to your situation and if your computer system will be able to include some of this information.

Will the inventory tracking system provide the accounting information you need?

Can the system track completed products as well as raw materials?

Will it be easy to take an inventory with the system?

Will you be able to relate reductions in inventory to specific sales, jobs, or products?

Will the system separate purchased items from produced items?

Will the system track work in progress?

☐ Decide which inventory system to use for accounting your inventory costs.

    ☐ Last in, first out (LIFO)

    ☐ First in, first out (FIFO)

    ☐ Average weighted cost

    ☐ Standard cost

☐ Determine when you will do a physical inventory.

    Will you have periodic cycle counts?

    Who will be responsible for doing these physical counts?

☐ Develop a reordering procedure for your business.

☐ Develop a system to alert you when to reorder.

☐ Develop a process to identify the most economical order quantities.

☐ Factor in lead-time for your reorder needs.

☐ Develop an identification system for your inventory items.

    Is it easily understood?

    Will you be able to put it into a computer program now or in the future?

    Will it fit the needs of the business as it grows or changes?

☐ Determine if you'll need to keep track of serial-numbered items. If so, how will you do so?

Business Management

Once you get your business up and running, you'll discover that start-up was the easy part of the business game! After operations and production have gotten underway, you'll find yourself playing the role of coach and manager in a myriad of issues and situations. Discovering your strengths and weaknesses as a biz leader and manager at this early point in your biz training should help you over any future management hurdles. And there will be hurdles!

This section helps you to gauge your thoughts and attitudes on a few management issues, including customer service, leadership skills, and turning a profit. Check out these management technique checklists and see where you stand on the biz playing field — are you a star quarterback or the water boy?

Customer Service Manager Checklist

To be in business means to serve the needs of your customers better than your competitors and inspire their loyalty and satisfaction. If you don't know how to handle service employees and policies now, you'll be watching customers leave right and left, and that's big trouble for any business.

Delivering Legendary Customer Service by Richard Gallagher talks about the service secrets that'll keep your future customers coming back as regulars. Here are some of the service tips he covers.

☐ Develop a strong rapport with your service staff by setting goals for their department and your business.

☐ Provide your service staff with quality, practical customer service training that'll help them succeed in their jobs.

☐ Set a good example of how you want your staff to treat customers.

☐ Create ways to keep your service staff motivated.

    ☐ Reward quality service skills and not just sales figures.

    ☐ Keep service standards well-known and very high.

    ☐ Provide regular doses of encouragement and inspiration.

    ☐ Give everyone a role in the service scheme of things.

☐ Prevent employee service burn-out.

    ☐ Don't overload staff members with too many chores and tasks.

    ☐ Be flexible on work shifts.

    ☐ Celebrate milestones with fun activities and perks.

    ☐ Encourage professional development.

☐ Investigate how to deal with problem service employees.

☐ Hire people with proven service skills, attitudes, and background.

    ☐ Check references.

    ☐ Get your service team involved.

☐ Know what your customers want and make sure you have it available.

☐ Learn how to build up, communicate, and inspire your service team organization.

☐ Coordinate customer-driven sales and marketing.

    ☐ Get to know your prospects as people.

☐ Sweat the details.

☐ Follow up after the sale.

☐ Continuously track your effectiveness in customer service.

    ☐ Learn from customer and employee feedback.

    ☐ Keep accurate records of all customer transactions.

Leadership Skills Checklist

Being team leader may or may not be your idea of having a good time, but when it comes to the business game, how you handle this role will greatly affect how your business will retain customers, employees, and a good reputation.

See if the checklist here on *The Leader's Guide* by Randall Ponder will help you in your quest and success as team leader.

☐ Understand your leadership style and attitude.

    Will you be democratic or autocratic?

    Will employees participate in decisions or not?

    How will you show enthusiasm, employee appreciation, etc.?

☐ Evaluate how you'll solve employee and other biz-related problems.

☐ Develop ways to manage your priorities.

    ☐ Analyze and control your time.

    ☐ Create ways to eliminate or reduce stress. (Have some fun!)

    ☐ Encourage open communication.

☐ Develop management techniques for projects.

    ☐ Select a good team to get the job done.

    ☐ Design, estimate, schedule, and budget for the project.

    ☐ Monitor the project's growth and progress.

    ☐ Have communication with all involved parties.

    ☐ Coordinate all follow-up activities.

☐ Promote staff training and development whenever possible.

    ☐ Determine training needs.

    ☐ Create mentor programs.

    ☐ Sponsor staff seminars and workshops.

- ☐ Strengthen your communications skills in any way possible.
    - ☐ Be approachable, understanding, and sincere.
    - ☐ Listen to others.
    - ☐ Be articulate in speech.
    - ☐ Deliver your message succinctly.
    - ☐ Write clearly.
    - ☐ Be aware of nonverbal communication.
    - ☐ Understand informal communication networks.
- ☐ Create strategies to motivate your employees and teams.
- ☐ Think ahead to how you'll solve conflicts, both internal and external.

Profit-Managing Techniques Checklist

Most of us think that if we get the customers in the door, the right price on the product or service, and the advertising on the radio that we're well on our way to turning a profit. But how do you go about managing your biz to increase profits? Well, that's what this checklist and the book, *People-Centered Profit Strategies* by Paul Peyton, try to tell you. See if any of these tips can work for you.

- ☐ Coach, counsel, and train your staff to be pro-profit.
    - ☐ Make employees feel comfortable and valued.
    - ☐ Generate excitement with promotions, incentives, and benefits.
    - ☐ Promote simplicity and a pro-profit attitude.
    - ☐ Get involved aggressively with willing and capable employees.
- ☐ Team up with pro-profit suppliers.
    - ☐ Seek the lowest total cost for what you need.
    - ☐ Help suppliers keep costs down.
    - ☐ Reduce the number of suppliers.
- ☐ Reward cost controls.
- ☐ Reverse sales declines, when they occur.
    - ☐ Find out what's causing them.
    - ☐ Anticipate market saturation.
    - ☐ Have a game plan for responding to competition.
    - ☐ Position your product so it stands above all the rest.

☐ Recognize when your business isn't operating efficiently.

 Are there any power struggles or hostilities going on?

Is management and employee morale low?

Are you over or understaffed?

☐ Set up an early warning system so you know when profits are slowing.

☐ Reduce your labor costs when needed.

☐ Reduce material costs.

☐ Apply wise pricing rules and strategies.

☐ Create strategies to stimulate quick cash flow.

> ☐ Close down a product line.
>
> ☐ Cleverly price a phaseout product. ˍ
>
> ☐ Focus on collecting past-due accounts.
>
> ☐ Discount overstocked items and inventory.
>
> ☐ Reduce overstaffing and inventory.
>
> ☐ Eliminate waste.

☐ Know the effect of raising prices and costs.

☐ Know the strength of your competition.

☐ Design ways to organize and monitor your business for cyclical ups and downs so you know what's coming in the short term.

Strategies and Tips

Playing the business game demands you put a lot of time into planning — planning everything from what media to advertise on to how much start-up inventory your business needs. All this planning will require your time and energy and probably the advice from business consultants or how-to business books. Obviously, production and management play a big part in your business' success and in satisfying your customers and employees, so get involved in this aspect of start-up research. Use the Plan of Action for Production and Management worksheet to organize and prioritize your thoughts.

- Develop a safety program for the procedures and operations in the warehouse. To obtain help for developing a safety program for your area, contact your workers' compensation insurer or your state's occupational safety and health agency.

- Constantly seek lower shipping rates and special billing arrangements. Quite frequently, trucking companies have heavy loads going in one direction, but they return unloaded. When this happens, they'll often give discounts on such routes.

- Consider having another company do your warehousing and shipping before you commit to leases, equipment, and inventory purchases.

- According to Bain and Company, a mere 5 percent increase in customer satisfaction levels can translate to as much as a staggering 85 percent increase in profitability.

- Good followers are a serious problem for poor leaders. They keep doing exactly what they're told! Make sure your communication skills are fine-tuned and you're organized in business management techniques.

Helpful Resources

Here are some good production and management resources to consider. For more of the same, you can refer to the appendices in the back of the book for info on SBDCs, biz magazines and other publications, and online resources for small business.

Ben & Jerry's Double Dip: Lead with Your Values and Make Money, Too
Simon & Schuster
(800) 223-2348

Sample the smooth and creamy advice these two entrepreneurs dish out on how to manage and lead your new biz.

Customer Service for Dummies
IDG Books
(312) 482-8346

Train your staff in how to deal with difficult people and situations and improve your personal communication skills.

Fundamentals of Inventory Management and Control
American Management Association (AMA)
1 (888) 281-5092

This practical, self-study course book gives you a thorough understanding of how inventory impacts the financial well-being of your company — as well as hands-on techniques to effectively manage inventory.

How to Plan and Manage Warehouse Operations
American Management Association (AMA)
1 (888) 281-5092

Covers all the elements to develop a sound management program for your warehouse. This course book introduces you to the kind of planning that maximizes the effective use of space, equipment, and labor.

Inventory Management
U.S. Small Business Administration
(800) 827-5722

This booklet discusses the purpose of inventory management, types of inventories, recordkeeping, and the role of forecasting.

National Association of Manufacturers (NAM)
(800) 736-6627 (Membership information)

The NAM is the voice for manufacturing in Washington, D.C., promoting a policy agenda that will increase the competitiveness of American industry. It also publishes a variety of booklets and publications that are very useful for the beginning or existing manufacturer.

Operations Management in Manufacturing
American Management Association (AMA)
1 (888) 281-5092

This self-study course book helps to identify the major stumbling blocks confronting operations management and presents a practical framework for overcoming them.

Uniform Code Council, Inc.
(937) 435-3870

To find out more about product bar codes, call the number above for advice and information.

Helpful Resources from The Oasis Press

The Oasis Press — The Leading Publisher of Small Business Information publishes some valuable management resources for the start-up biz owner. See if any look interesting for your new biz. You can order these books from your local bookstore, or call the company directly at:

The Oasis Press
(800) 228-2275

Delivering Legendary Customer Service: Seven Steps to Success

Get the skinny on what it takes to be a customer service manager and get, keep, and increase customers for life.

Information Breakthrough

Find out how to sift through all the details of your biz and find the gems of useful information that'll keep your biz flying high and strong.

The Leader's Guide: 15 Essential Skills

Inspire loyalty, commitment, and drive in your staff and others by learning essential leadership skills.

People-Centered Profit Strategies: 101 Competitive Advantages

Learn about the ups and downs of biz and how to survive and strategize during each ebb and flow.

Renaissance 2000: Liberal Arts Essentials for Tomorrow's Leaders

Cultivate your leadership skills from an unexpected source — the liberal arts!

Strategic Management for Small and Growing Firms

Become an effective planner and learn the in's and out's of managing a small business. Gain insights from the numerous case studies and build up your self-confidence for managing your business in the 21st century.

Surviving Success: Surviving the Challenges of Growth

A savvy book on how to take your biz to the next level without slipping back. Studies biz leader secrets for overcoming barriers and expanding enterprise. A good management techniques resource.

Notes

_____

_____

_____

_____

_____

_____

_____

_____

_____

_____

_____

_____

_____

_____

_____

_____

_____

_____

_____

_____

_____

_____

_____

_____

_____

_____

Plan of Action for Production and Management

Your company will be producing a:
☐ Product   ☐ Service

Use this planning tool to organize and prioritize the activities in this chapter that you've checked off. Don't feel you have to list all the activities you've checked off. Simply start with the top ten most important ones and go from there, or do whatever is easiest for you. Make plenty of copies of this cut-out worksheet for your planning and organizing activities for this chapter.

Action to be Taken	Begin Date	Who	Deadline

Plan of Action (continued)

Action to be Taken	Begin Date	Who	Deadline

Chapter 6

Environmental Options and Laws

Introduction

The recent tide of environmental opinions and concerns has changed the way many businesses function. Regardless of what you may think about the earth's environmental health, public and personal opinion — and even current state and federal laws — will most likely dictate how you operate your business so it's more environment-friendly.

As a result of the recent environmental movement, the U.S. government has passed more than a dozen environmental laws. The most prominent of these laws are:

- The Comprehensive Environmental Response, Compensation and Liability Act (CERCLA), or more commonly known as the Superfund law;
- The Hazardous Materials Transportation Act (HMTA);
- The National Environmental Protection Act (NEPA); and
- The Resource Conservation and Recovery Act (RCRA).

The other laws cover safety and health; water, air, and noise pollution; and wildlife. In addition to these, most states have their own set of environmental laws. It'll be your responsibility as a new business owner to find out which local, state, and federal environmental laws pertain to your particular product or service. Remember that environmental law is a dynamic area — what's merely an option today may be a law tomorrow.

With this thought in mind, this chapter provides tips for you to start developing a cost-effective environmental plan for your new business, in addition to helping you be aware of some of the current environmental requirements that apply to all businesses. The chapter takes you through the five R's of managing your business materials to dealing with hazardous materials legally and safely. The chapter concludes with a section on how to increase your energy and resource efficiency.

First Aid for Environmental Concerns

 *The Business Environmental Handbook* by Martin D. Westerman is a comprehensive book that leads you step-by-step through the process of developing an environmental plan to make your business more efficient. This book shows you how to be environment-friendly. Much of the information in this chapter is drawn from *The Business Environmental Handbook*. You may purchase this book from any local bookstore or order directly from the publisher.

The Business Environmental Handbook
The Oasis Press
(800) 228-2275

Getting Started

Many opportunities to make your business environment-friendly are available in today's pro-environment atmosphere. However, don't try to do all the activities mentioned in this chapter at once. Developing an environmental plan is most likely an optional activity for you at this point in time, and simply taking the time to learn more about it is a step in the right direction. Start with the checklist activities that are the easiest and most convenient for you to implement, and go from there.

By thinking about ways to conserve and recycle now, you can be better prepared for any future legislation that may affect how you run your business. In addition to being better prepared, it really does pay to conserve and recycle. Your business can cut costs on energy bills and office supplies, plus you can earn money by producing extra energy or selling recyclable items.

A big part of any environmental plan is how well you manage the materials you'll use for producing your product or performing your service, plus the materials you'll use in everyday business operations, such as paper, gas, and electricity. Effectively managing your materials can reduce your waste and disposal costs by at least 30 percent. To successfully manage your materials and to begin formulating your own environmental plan, incorporate the five environmental R's into your business practices. The five R's are rethink, reduce, reuse, recycle, and results. The fifth R is achieved by carrying out the first four.

The five R's each have their own checklist of activities in this section. They follow the Getting Started Checklist listed below. Use these checklists to develop a cost-cutting, money-saving environmental plan for your new business.

Getting Started Checklist

The hardest part of any endeavor is getting started. As you begin thinking about an environmental plan for your new business, consider the strengths and limitations of your suppliers, locality, facility, and staff. All these factors will influence which actions you choose to carry out in your environmental plan. The checklist below will help you address the preliminary considerations for creating your plan.

☐ Create a company environmental mission statement, and include it as a policy in your company manual.

 Are you going to take an active part in helping the environment, such as sponsoring community clean-up or tree-planting projects?

Or, are you going to limit your environmental actions to simply ensuring that your company practices do not harm the environment?

☐ Demonstrate support for your environmental plan to your employees and suppliers. Options could include that you:

  ☐ Offer bonuses or other incentives to employees who suggest environment-friendly changes in company practices.

  ☐ Prepare a letter that states your preferences in packing materials and packaging, and send it to your suppliers.

☐ Encourage any future employees to look for wastes and suggest any improvements.

☐ Determine if your suppliers can provide you with recycled or environment-friendly materials.

☐ Research the recycling and composting options available in your area.

> Is there a recycling or composting program available? If so, what are the requirements to participate?
>
> Are there any composting requirements for your state? Check with your state's environmental protection agency.

☐ Ask your utility company if it provides conservation kits. If so, get one.

☐ Determine the limitations of your facility, such as the amount of indoor and outdoor space available for recycling or composting.

☐ Consider writing a policy outlining your commitment to the environment and each employee's responsibility to uphold this commitment. Include the policy in your company policy manual.

☐ Start with low-cost/no-cost measures, such as providing ceramic mugs to employees rather than disposable cups for hot coffee or tea.

Rethink Checklist

By simply thinking through how your day-to-day activities will operate, you can discover many areas where you can make changes that will be environment-friendly. If you do an operations section for a business plan, this information would be very impressive to include, and any potential investor would note your extra effort. (See Chapter 7.) Also, if you are creating a business plan, but are only in the research stage, be sure to file your findings from the activities listed in this checklist in your business plan file for future reference. The activities below provide options for you to consider.

☐ Think about how your business will operate, and determine what will be thrown away and why.

    ☐ Eliminate, revalue, or reorient materials that will be thrown out.

☐ Make a diagram depicting the flow of materials from where they will enter your business to where they will exit. Make a separate diagram for each process and procedure.

    ☐ Determine if all the products and materials you anticipate using are really necessary to your business.

    ☐ Examine the possibility of consolidating or eliminating steps, based on the diagram.

☐ Purchase supplies with minimum packaging materials.

☐ Request your suppliers to use recyclable or biodegradable packaging wherever applicable.

☐ Research how your business can produce less waste for your customers once you are up and running.

For example, if you are producing a product, are you using the least amount of packing materials possible?

Reduce Checklist

Source reduction — reducing the amount of materials you use for a particular project — is the key to reducing your waste output. Source reduction alone can cut your waste output by 10 to 30 percent. Some source reduction options are provided for you in the activities below.

☐ Purchase materials in bulk quantities whenever possible to eliminate excessive container and packaging waste.

☐ Make two-sided photocopies to reduce the amount of paper used.

☐ Remove your company name from unwanted mailing lists so your junk mail is reduced.

☐ Estimate equipment usage and rent or borrow, rather than buy, items you will rarely use.

☐ Plan to use biodegradable, recyclable, reusable, or no packing materials whenever possible.

Reuse Checklist

Reusing materials rather than buying new ones is an excellent way to help reduce waste, cut business expenses, and implement an environment-friendly activity.

The activities below will give you some ideas on where to start. This checklist is brief, but it gives you some clues as to what to look for. Be sure to evaluate your particular business for other opportunities to reuse materials.

☐ Furnish your office with pre-owned, quality equipment wherever possible.

☐ Use the blank side of used paper for messages and scratch pads.

☐ Reuse packing materials or return them to the supplier.

☐ Investigate starting a materials exchange program — both in-house and with other businesses in your location.

> Can waste materials from one department be put to good use in another? For example, if one department generates paper as waste, bind it into scratch pads for other departments, such as accounting, to use.
>
> Do you generate waste materials that another company can use? For example, your old wooden pallets can be useful to a company that produces mulch from wood.

☐ Reuse materials, such as file folders and inter-office envelopes, as often as possible.

☐ Recharge printer cartridges and re-ink printer ribbons.

Recycling and Composting Checklist

Recycling and composting are two methods you can use to reduce your waste disposal costs. Many states encourage recycling efforts. Check with your local and state authorities to determine what, if any, of the following activities are optional or required for your business location. This checklist will get you to thinking about your recycling and composting efforts.

☐ Plan to purchase recycled-content materials to stimulate the recycling market.

☐ Decide what materials your business will recycle.

☐ Research your local recycling options.

> What materials are recycled in your area?
>
> Do recyclers require a minimum amount of materials?
>
> Do recyclers charge to pick up materials?
>
> Do recyclers pay for materials?

☐ Estimate the types and quantities of recyclable materials your business will generate.

☐ Calculate the potential savings or profits from recycling.

☐ Consider purchasing a compactor if you will generate 1,000 pounds or more of cardboard per week.

☐ Develop a recycling policy to include in your company policy manual.

☐ Provide adequate space for your recycling or composting operation. Consider:

How much material do you plan to recycle or compost per week?

What types of material will you recycle?

Does your state require landscape trimmings and other compostable materials to be separated out of regular garbage? (Nearly 30 states require that you do.)

How often will recyclable materials be picked up or delivered?

☐ Place recycling boxes near copy machines, fax machines, and computer printers, so it's convenient to put paper in them.

☐ Consider composting if your business will generate a pound or more of "wet" garbage per day and it's acceptable within your zoning guidelines. See the Glossary for a definition of wet garbage.

Hazardous Materials

A hazardous material is defined as any material or substance that is caustic, flammable, corrosive, reactive, or toxic. This covers a wide range of materials, including highly publicized toxins, banned pesticides, and even everyday household items, such as a can of Raid.

You're responsible for any hazardous material you use in your business and any damage it may cause. There is no statute of limitations on the damage caused by hazardous materials. For example, if you form a corporation that's later dissolved, under the Superfund law, officers and shareholders continue to be liable for any environmental damage caused by the corporation's hazardous materials.

This section provides two checklists to help you handle hazardous materials successfully and legally and reduce your liability.

The checklist activities that are required by law for all companies that handle hazardous materials are followed by an (R), which stands for "required." Some of the activities in the checklists are presented as options, yet may be required for some companies — the determining factor is how much hazardous waste your company will generate and how toxic the waste will be. Again, be sure to do your business game homework here. Find out what applies or does not apply to your business.

For more information on the legalities of handling hazardous materials, refer to *The Business Environmental Handbook,* the U.S. Environmental Protection Agency (EPA), and your state and local environmental departments.

Successfully Handling Hazardous Materials Checklist

Hazardous materials can cause harm to areas far outside the area of intended use. Not only can hazardous materials affect employee health, insurance costs, and real estate transactions, they can also increase your liability to the community at large. This checklist will help you set up procedures for successfully handling hazardous materials that are necessary for your business process.

- ☐ Create a written statement that clearly identifies your company's policies and objectives pertaining to handling hazardous materials and include the policies in your employee handbook.

- ☐ Plan to select a coordinator or committee to assess hazardous material inputs and outputs once your business is up and running.

- ☐ Set up a recordkeeping system and maintain a log of all actions and efforts pertaining to hazardous materials. (R)

- ☐ Determine which category of hazardous waste generator (listed below) your business will be considered. These definitions are set by federal law. For more information, contact your local solid waste management department or your regional office of the EPA.

  - ☐ Household or conditionally exempt small quantity generator

  - ☐ Moderate or medium quantity generator

  - ☐ Large quantity generator

- ☐ Research the laws and reporting requirements for your level of hazardous waste generation.

  - ☐ Compile a list of required permits and other environmental requirements from all local agencies.

- ☐ Contact your local solid waste management department and ask about disposal options, if you're a conditionally exempt small quantity generator. If you're a moderate and large quantity generators, you must comply with federal laws.

- ☐ Rethink how your business will operate and eliminate or reduce the amount of hazardous materials used, wherever possible.

☐ Obtain American LabelMark's Hazardous Materials Identification System (HMIS®) labels for all hazardous materials you will use. (This is one way to satisfy federal OSHA's hazardous communication standard requirements.)

☐ Investigate creating in-house programs and participating in out-of-house programs for reusing hazardous wastes, such as chemical compounds, solvents, lubricants, and coatings.

☐ Make arrangements to utilize local recycling programs for materials such as oil and antifreeze.

☐ Create an in-house means or hire a licensed contractor to detoxify or neutralize hazardous wastes. (R)

☐ Schedule a review of your business practices before you open your business.

    ☐ Look for areas where hazardous materials can be further reduced.

    ☐ Look for any areas or uses that could cause you to be held liable for damages.

Controlling Your Exposure to Liability Checklist

This checklist will help you reduce your exposure to liability for hazardous materials; however, the laws governing hazardous materials are constantly evolving, so you'll need to stay aware of current legislative activity.

This checklist is in no way comprehensive. It's merely intended to make you aware of the types of requirements you'll need to comply with once your business is up and running. Be sure to check with your local authorities, and with your regional office of the EPA, to find out exactly which laws apply to your company.

☐ Research discharging and reporting requirements for hazardous materials and be sure that you comply with every requirement. Do not take shortcuts or overlook even the smallest detail. (R)

Be aware that if you discharge hazardous materials illegally and then file false reports, you may be prosecuted under the Racketeering Influenced and Corrupt Organizations (RICO) Act.

☐ Check the legality of selling or transferring hazardous materials before doing so. (R)

☐ Set up a check system to ensure that all hazardous substances have been properly treated before they are discharged. (R)

☐ Obtain the services of a licensed and bonded contractor to transport and dispose of your hazardous wastes. (R) (You may be able to obtain a license to do this yourself, but doing so will increase your liability.)

    ☐ Require proof that the contractor meets all legal requirements.

    ☐ Ask for references and check the reputation of the contractor.

☐ Post or centrally locate Material Safety Data Sheets (MSDSs) for all hazardous materials your business will handle. (R)

    ☐ Contact your local occupational safety and health office for more information on MSDSs.

    ☐ Train each employee who will handle hazardous materials about how to understand and use the information on the MSDSs.

Increase Your Energy and Resource Efficiency

This may come as a surprise to you, but utility companies are all too happy to help you increase your energy efficiency. It's cheaper for them to help you install efficient energy and water systems than it is for them to find and develop new sources of energy and water. Many offer free services and low- or no-cost loans to help you install energy- and water-efficient equipment. This section provides checklists for energy, water, and transportation efficiency measures. Consider implementing some of these optional measures into your environmental plan.

Energy Efficiency Checklist

You can "create" energy for your business by investing in efficient equipment and cutting waste. Every function of your business you improve, and every energy waste you eliminate, is money in your pocket.

☐ Make energy efficiency a company policy.

☐ Determine the most cost-effective sources of energy for your business.

    ☐ Compare the rates from different sources of energy in your area, such as solar power, hydro-electric power, natural gas, coal, or oil-fired power plants.

☐ Install window films, shades, or curtains on all windows to block the sun's heat during the hot season. This will help reduce the power needed for air conditioning.

☐ Ask your local utility companies what assistance programs they offer for making your business more energy efficient.

☐ Investigate using solar thermal units for space and water heating.

☐ Install water heater jackets where appropriate, and insulate hot water piping throughout your building(s).

☐ Preset heating and air conditioning thermostats, and turn water heater, refrigeration, and freezer thermostats to the minimums allowable for health codes and energy conservation.

☐ Use task lighting for work areas and stations — that is, place lamps on individual desks and over copy holders for computers rather than using overhead lights to light an entire room.

☐ Turn off or "standby" all lights and equipment when they are not in use.

☐ Use daylighting as much as possible. See the Glossary for a definition.

  ☐ Install interior lights that will automatically dim or shut off when bright daylight is available.

☐ Install only energy-efficient lighting fixtures.

☐ Install dimmers, occupancy sensors, timers, or trip switches to reduce energy usage.

☐ Investigate cogeneration. See the Glossary.

Water Efficiency Checklist

By using water efficiency measures, you can cut your business' water consumption by up to 25 percent a year. The activities below will help you use your water efficiently and save money.

☐ Make efficient water use a company policy.

☐ Review all activities and processes for water efficiency.

☐ Install low-flow or laminar flow aerators at all sink faucets.

☐ Install low-flow shower heads with on-off flow interrupters, if you're going to provide showers for your employees.

☐ Install ultra-low flush toilets.

☐ Xeriscape. In other words, landscape with drought-tolerant flora appropriate for your climate.

☐ Use positive shut-off nozzles on all hoses.

☐ Water the landscape only when needed.

    ☐ Water only in the mornings and evenings, on overcast days, or when the area to be watered is in the shade.

☐ Check to see if you can use greywater for irrigation purposes.

☐ Use standing or drag-out rinses, extra tanks for cascade rinsing, or counter-current rinsing wherever appropriate for manufacturing processes.

Transportation Options Checklist

Everybody in business has to get to and from work, transport a product, or meet with customers. As you make plans to start your business, consider the cost-saving transportation options and alternatives presented in the activities below. They may provide you with some money-saving measures. These activities are optional and are simply provided for your review and consideration.

☐ Create a transportation utilization list to help you understand what your transportation needs will be.

    ☐ List each vehicle or form of transportation you'll use.

    ☐ After each vehicle, write a description, considering the following:

        Where will you use your vehicles?

        What will they cost you?

        Are your intended vehicles the best to use for your tasks?

        Will your vehicles carry optimum loads?

☐ Minimize your vehicles' environmental impacts by performing proper maintenance procedures.

☐ Explore uses of alternative vehicle types and fuel or power sources for specific purposes in your business.

☐ Create an employee commute-trip-reduction program.

    ☐ Provide free or discounted public transit passes to your employees to encourage public transit use.

    ☐ Post public transit schedules.

    ☐ Offer incentives to carpoolers, such as free parking or a cash bonus.

    ☐ Provide a guaranteed ride home for carpoolers who have to work late or leave for domestic emergencies.

- ☐ Consider providing an on-site day care facility. Besides reducing gas consumption, it also is beneficial for reducing employee time off and turnover and promoting employee morale and productivity.

- ☐ Encourage employees who live nearby to ride their bicycles or walk to work.

    - ☐ Provide showers and a safe place to store bicycles for employees who wish to bicycle to work.

- ☐ Consider telecommuting as an alternative for those employees whose position it applies to. This way, those employees would not have to physically commute to the office every day.

Strategies and Tips

 As you have seen from the activities listed in this chapter, being environment-friendly can actually save you money and in some instances, increase your profits. Here are some additional tips for maintaining an environment-friendly business. A listing of resources you may find helpful is included after the tips.

- Stay informed about environmental issues pertaining to business in general.
- If you can generate excess electricity, your local utility company is required to purchase the excess from you.
- Create your own environmental business practices before you are required to do so by law. It will be much more cost-effective to stay ahead of environmental regulations than to play catch up.
- Avoid the use of hazardous materials as much as possible.
- Document all your environment-friendly actions for future use in a business plan or company promotion.
- Take advantage of green marketing opportunities. Refer to *The Business Environmental Handbook* for more information on green marketing.

Helpful Resources

Here are some environmental-related resources for you to consider. For more of the same, you can refer to the appendices in the back of the book for info on SBDCs, biz magazines and other publications, and online resources for small business.

BioCycle
J.G. Press, Inc.
(610) 967-4135

A monthly magazine on solid waste management with an emphasis on composting. Call for subscription information.

Business Guide to Waste Reduction & Recycling
Xerox Documentation Subscription Service
(800) 327-9753

A handy guide that offers information on waste reduction and recycling, especially for businesses.

A Guide to Resource Efficient Building Elements
Center for Resourceful Building Technology
(406) 549-7678

A handy guide for making your building more efficient.

Hazardous Materials Identification System (HMIS)
American LabelMark/Labelmaster
(800) 621-5808

This company provides the colorful HMIS labels, which include a personal protection index. They also provide training materials. Write or call for more information.

Real Goods, Inc.
(707) 468-9292

Real Goods is a catalog supplier of environment-friendly products and equipment. It also publishes the *Alternative Energy Sourcebook* and various books focusing on the environment and related issues. Call for ordering information.

Seventh Generation
(800) 456-1197

This company is a catalog supplier of environment-friendly products and equipment. Call to request a catalog.

Small Business Ombudsman
U.S. Environmental Protection Agency
(800) 368-5888

Provides help and assistance to small businesses trying to comply with the Clean Air Act and other environmental requirements.

Solid Waste Composting Council
(301) 913-2885

Contact this organization for more information on composting solid wastes.

Helpful Resources from The Oasis Press

The Oasis Press — The Leading Publisher of Small Business Information publishes a one-stop environmental, biz-related book for the start-up biz owner. You can order this book from your local bookstore, or call the company directly at:

The Oasis Press
(800) 228-2275

The Business Environmental Handbook

Gives you a headstart as an environmentally savvy business. Has you create and ponder strategies that will recycle and reduce waste, comply with state and federal laws, and save money!

Notes

_____

_____

_____

_____

_____

_____

_____

_____

_____

_____

_____

_____

_____

_____

_____

_____

_____

_____

_____

_____

_____

_____

_____

_____

_____

_____

_____

_____

Plan of Action for Environmental Options and Laws

Your company will:

☐ Develop a recycling program
☐ Get ideas on how to save on energy costs

☐ Review applicable laws
☐ Investigate environmental issues in your industry

Use this planning tool to organize and prioritize the activities in this chapter that you've checked off. Don't feel you have to list all the activities you've checked off. Simply start with the top ten most important ones and go from there, or do whatever is easiest for you. Make plenty of copies of this cut-out worksheet for your planning and organizing activities for this chapter.

Action to be Taken	Begin Date	Who	Deadline

Plan of Action (continued)

Action to be Taken	Begin Date	Who	Deadline
_____	_____	_____	_____
_____	_____	_____	_____
_____	_____	_____	_____
_____	_____	_____	_____
_____	_____	_____	_____
_____	_____	_____	_____
_____	_____	_____	_____
_____	_____	_____	_____
_____	_____	_____	_____
_____	_____	_____	_____
_____	_____	_____	_____
_____	_____	_____	_____
_____	_____	_____	_____
_____	_____	_____	_____
_____	_____	_____	_____
_____	_____	_____	_____
_____	_____	_____	_____
_____	_____	_____	_____
_____	_____	_____	_____
_____	_____	_____	_____
_____	_____	_____	_____
_____	_____	_____	_____
_____	_____	_____	_____
_____	_____	_____	_____
_____	_____	_____	_____

Chapter 7

Writing a Start-Up Business Plan

Introduction

Business plans are like game plans; they help you scout out information on your business and then help you strategize your way to the winner's circle. Most often, they're used for requesting financing from bankers and venture capitalists. Investors want to see financial information and bottom lines on paper to help them make their decision on whether or not to fund a new venture or business.

In recent years, business plans have also become more of an all-purpose internal biz tool that features many other facets of doing business. In addition to financial specifics, business plans include information on overall goal-setting; defining the business; reviewing business operations; collecting industry and marketing data; and evaluating new products, competition, and growth. In this new millennium, business plans will also be redefined and redesigned to meet the growing demands of biz plan readers who want shorter, more focused information.

Even though writing a business plan takes time, thought, and effort, many business owners have discovered how valuable it is to have all this information at their fingertips before opening their doors. Even if you won't be requesting funds in the beginning, you'll make better decisions and understand your business' strengths and weaknesses if you have done a business plan. You'll enter the biz game better prepared and ready for the rigors of running a small business.

But undertaking the task of writing a business plan may seem like running a marathon to you! Hang in there! With some discipline and the help of this chapter, you can begin the process of writing your own business plan that's specifically for a start-up business. Like training for a marathon, it's a day-to-day process that builds on itself, making you stronger and savvier along the way.

First Aid for Writing Your Start-Up Business Plan

 Nearly all the information in this chapter comes from *The Rule Book of Business Plans for Startups* by Roger C. Rule. This business plan book is head and shoulders above the others because it's written just for start-up businesses. If you're new to the biz game and unfamiliar with the business plan writing plan process, this book's for you! Get start-up business plan samples (and advice) for various business types, such as a manufacturing and assembly company, a service business, a home office business, and a retail or wholesale company. Plus learn how to structure your plan as a planning or capital-raising tool. The book is available through your local bookstore, or you can order it directly from the publisher.

The Rule Book of Business Plans for Startups
The Oasis Press
(800) 228-2275

Handy appendices also help you calculate key biz ratios and find financing sources for your budding business.

Business Plan Preliminaries

Let's get warmed up to the idea of writing a business plan with some basic assumptions. So, before sharpening your pencil and rolling up your sleeves, hopefully you've done and know the following:

- You're in the starting blocks and ready to go into business.
- You have your basic business concept defined.
- You've decided on your basic products and services.
- You've selected your location and facility.
- You've retained a business accountant and attorney.
- You understand your financial position and your investment costs.

If you don't have one of these basic warm-up exercises figured out yet, then do some more workouts before moving on in the business plan process. These basic issues get explored even more in later business plan activities. For example, you'll be evaluating business objectives, mission statements, industry and market analyses, and management strategies — just to name a few. So get these basic beginning exercises completed as soon as you can.

Other start-up business plan prelims to cover include a how to create a professional first impression.

First Impressions Checklist

You only get one chance to make a good first impression. And with so much competition for start-up dollars, make your plan neat, accurate, and professional-looking so you stand out above the crowd. Before you begin, consider ways you can do this.

☐ Take a trip to your local print shop and decide what type of binding format you can best use for your plan.

☐ Decide if you'll go the extra mile and have printed covers or printed binding strips for your business plan booklet.

☐ Design a consistent page layout that is balanced and artistically pleasing.

　　☐ Use the latest desktop publishing software tools for help with borders, shadow lines, and boxes.

　　☐ Use an easy-to-read font.

☐ Create tabs for each titled heading in your business plan.

☐ Use colored partitions to coordinate with other colors in graphs or charts.

☐ Choose three or four rich colors and use them consistently throughout your work. (It beats black and white and will make your plan more dynamic.)

☐ Print your plan using laser or ink-jet printers only.

☐ Select either bright white or stationery-quality paper.

☐ Find a good proofreader or editor to doublecheck your writing and your figures.

Preliminary Papers Checklist

Like a book or formal report, your business plan will feature a few introductory pages — such as a customized cover letter; a confidentiality agreement, if necessary; a title page; and a table of contents. These intro pages are meant to spark interest in your start-up and urge readers to continue. They'll also show readers your organization and professionalism.

☐ Research business plan cover letter samples to get a feel for what to include and how to approach your respective readers.

☐ Write drafts of several cover letters that grab attention, discuss your main points concisely, and include and explain important figures.

☐ Customize each of your cover letters to their respective recipients, including names, titles, and company address. Always proofread to ensure accuracy of names, dates, etc.

☐ Decide if you'll want or need a confidentiality or non-disclosure agreement created for your use.

☐ Remember to include a title page —immediately following the plan's cover sheet — that features all the necessary information, including, among other items, the date and your (and the recipient's) name, title, business name, and address. Arrange the page in a professional, clear page layout.

☐ Table of contents follows the title page and should be clear as to the organization of the plan's sections and exhibits.

Your Business Plan's Sections and Outline

Any business plan book worth its salt will give you strong reasons for writing a business plan, but few explain the thinking behind why its sections are organized a certain way. There are three basic purposes to structuring a business plan's sections.

1. To organize the sections in their importance to your company;
2. To organize the sections in their importance to the reviewer, once you know who that person will be; and
3. To organize the sections in the order of the logical development of your company.

While the first two have their merits for existing companies, the best approach for a start-up business plan is the logical development option. Here, you arrange the biz plan sections in a logical manner to clearly tell the story of how your start-up company has been designed. After smoothly telling the story, have the plan climax with the final dollar figures and your financial request.

Keeping this secret formula in mind, here's the savvy structure and sections to include in your start-up business plan.

- Executive summary
- Company description
- Industry analysis
- The market and competition
- Strategies and goals
- Products or services
- Marketing and sales
- Management and organization
- Operations
- Financial pro formas
- Financial requirement
- Exhibits

While a business plan can be a terrific tool for setting direction and improving company efficiency, most start-ups use them for obtaining financing. So that's why you have the financial information towards the end. Hopefully, by the time readers get done reviewing your smoothly written, logical story, they're ready to listen to your financial request.

The following checklists are presented in the order you'd want to present in your start-up business plan. First up to bat, executive summary!

Executive Summary Checklist

The buck stops here. Of all the business plan sections, this one is by far the most important because it's the only section you can expect all of the reviewers to read, and it's always the first section to be read. If your executive summary is not well-written and powerful enough in message, readers stop in their tracks, and the rest of your plan gets ignored.

- [ ] Keep your executive summary to one or two pages in length for a thirty-page plan. (Three pages is okay for a forty-page plan, but remember, the shorter, the better.)

- [ ] Write concisely; make every word count.

- [ ] Make material interesting and vibrant, but don't exaggerate.

- [ ] Be objective and establish credibility right away with your reader.

- [ ] Write an initial draft of your executive summary before researching and writing your business plan. Keep it for later reference.

☐ Emphasize only the most essential details of your start-up.

☐ Decide on a review-style or preview-style format for your executive summary.

> A review format covers all the sections of the business plan, but on a "mini" scale.
>
> The preview format is written in a more narrative style covering the important highlights of the plan.

☐ Revise your initial draft and write the final draft of the executive summary after you've completely finished your plan.

Company Description Checklist

After the executive summary, reviewers have taken a peek inside your start-up. Now, it's time to invite them in to have a look around. The company description section is one of the easiest sections to write because there's no calculating or major research to do. So have fun here and think about what you'd like to say about your new start-up biz. Here's what to include in your writing.

☐ Introduce your company's name, whether it's the legal name, popular name, or the doing-business-as name.

☐ Write an inviting narrative paragraph that explains your business concept. Briefly identify the following:

  ☐ Your industry;

  ☐ Your business specialty;

  ☐ Your target market;

  ☐ Your product and services;

  ☐ Your niche compared to the competition; and

  ☐ At least one long-term business goal.

> What business are you in?
>
> What do you sell and to whom?
>
> Do you have a trend market, niche market, or customer-focused market?
>
> What are your product or service's special features and benefits?
>
> Where do you see your business in ten years?

☐ Indicate your form of ownership, for example, sole proprietor, partnership, or corporation.

☐ State the name and title of the person running the show.

☐ List the business address(es).

☐ Describe one or two main reasons why your location is important to your business.

_____

_____

_____

_____

_____

_____

_____

☐ Explain your geographic sales area, any strategic alliances, and vital physical descriptions, if any.

_____

_____

_____

_____

_____

_____

_____

☐ Write about the current status of your start-up and any major milestones you've accomplished.

_____

_____

_____

_____

_____

_____

_____

Industry Analysis Checklist

Well, just the term alone is enough to stop you in your tracks! But you might be pleasantly surprised at how easy and interesting gathering this information might be for you. A well-stocked library and the Internet can make this section easier and faster to write. And this checklist will let you know what to research. An industry analysis section is considered a necessity for a start-up's business plan. So don't skimp on this part of your biz game workout!

☐ Obtain the numerical code for your business' Standard Industry Classification (SIC) via the U.S. Census Bureau.

☐ Obtain the newer codes — the North American Industry Classification System (NAICS) — from the U.S. Census Bureau.

☐ Once you know your codes, look for revenues, total units of products or services sold, and total employees for your sector in all levels (national, state, county, city).

☐ Know the gross domestic product (GDP) and gross state product (GSP) growth rates. Be prepared to make comparisons.

☐ Write an industry summary paragraph that highlights significant points in this entire section. (It's best to write this summary last, after completing your research.) This summary includes:

    ☐ The best or unique features of the industry description (See below.);

    ☐ Your business' economic sector;

    ☐ A description of your sector's growth;

    ☐ An explanation of your industry and a comparison of its size and rate of growth compared to the GDP;

    ☐ An indication of your industry's level of maturation;

    ☐ A discussion of any trends that affect your industry; and

    ☐ An explanation of industry opportunities that you foresee as important to your future business.

☐ Write an industry description.

    ☐ Identify your NAICS and SIC numbers.

    ☐ Provide the Census Bureau's economic sector description for your industry.

    ☐ Include your industry's total sales in terms of dollars nationwide for the most recent year.

- ☐ Mention the competition within your industry.
- ☐ Describe a common profile of companies in your industry.
- ☐ Discuss any significant changes occurring in your industry.
- ☐ Discuss your industry size and maturation.

> What is the size of your economic sector in the United States?
>
> What is its growth rate?
>
> What is the size and growth rate of your industry overall?

- ☐ Identify and discuss impact factors for your industry.
- ☐ Explain industry standards and obstacles.
- ☐ Write a paragraph on findings that affect your industry's opportunities.

The Market and Competition Checklist

This is an extremely valuable section of your business plan because you'll get to know your future customers extremely well. And knowing what they want and why — and determining how you'll deliver the goods better than the competition — will help give you a strong start in business. Here's a checklist to get your research juices flowing.

- ☐ Write a market and competition summary to introduce this section's main highlights and factors.
- ☐ Determine your market's segmentation (See Glossary for definition.)
- ☐ Determine which of these market segments is your target market.
    - ☐ Analyze your target market thoroughly by determining the percentages of customer types for your new business, for example, individual consumers vs. commercial customers.
    - ☐ Research demographic data on your consumers or target market.

> What is the percentage of males and females?
>
> How old is your average customer?
>
> Are they mostly single or married individuals?
>
> What's their annual household income, occupation, and education levels?
>
> Do they own or rent?

    - ☐ Research the psychographics of your target market. (See Glossary.)

☐ Write about your consumers' geographic area, for example, on a national, regional, state, or city basis.

☐ Once you've researched much of the above data, write a consumer profile — that is, describe the gender, age, income, interests, etc. of your "average" consumer.

☐ Research as much as possible on your competition, whether they're franchises, chain stores, or independents.

☐ Identify all of your competitors by company name within your sales area.

☐ Single out your main competitors and analyze their strengths and weaknesses.

☐ Determine your market share.

☐ Discuss your market's obstacles for new businesses.

☐ Highlight what unique and probable opportunities your market will offer your start-up.

Strategies and Goals Checklist

In this section, you'll be letting others know about your long-term goals for the business, as well as stating your strategies for positioning your company or products or services, or both, in the marketplace. Since investors are looking for long-term gains, this is a vital section to capture their attention and gain their confidence in you.

☐ Write a strategies summary highlighting all of the important goals and strategies you develop in this section. (Write this paragraph after completing your research.)

☐ Define your long-term goals and strategies.

Are you price-driven, service-driven, or customer service-driven? Where do you see your business in three, five, and ten years? What's your strategies for getting there?

☐ Write a brief statement about the various methods you'll use to implement your strategies and meet your long-term goals.

Products or Services Checklist

This is the section where readers get an upfront and personal look at your products and services. If your products and services are unique and very intriguing, be thorough and lively in your descriptions so you pique the reader's attention. If, however, your products or services aren't unusual, be succinct and clear, and then move on. Here's what to include in this section of your start-up business plan.

☐ Write a products or services summary.

☐ Write a products or services description.

    ☐ Mention price, upgrades, important features and benefits.

☐ Include a brief statement of how your products or services will be positioned in the marketplace.

> Will you be the lowest priced?
>
> Do you have the most technical design?
>
> Will you be filling a marketing niche?

☐ Discuss how your products or services compare to your competitions' products or services.

☐ If your products or services have intellectual protection, such as a trademark, trade name, service mark, patent, or copyright, list it and give an explanation as to who owns what.

Marketing and Sales Checklist

Any good marketing and sales section of a start-up business plan includes a marketing summary, strategy, plan, and budget. In addition, it features an advertising plan and a discussion on the sales force and sales forecast. In it, you detail how you'll reach your target market, convey your message and motivate them to buy, and generate sales.

☐ Write your marketing and sales summary. (Written after you complete all this research.)

☐ Research and compile information for your marketing strategy.

☐ Determine what message you will send to your target market. This message should inform the consumers on:

    ☐ What your products or services are and their benefits/features;

    ☐ The price you're asking for your products or services;

    ☐ Where they buy your products or services; and

    ☐ A promotional value that's added to your products or services.

☐ Develop a business promotion that focuses on one or two of your main product or service benefits. (Many biz owners create a slogan to convey this message.)

☐ Develop a complete marketing plan.

  ☐ Determine how much you can budget to implement your marketing plan.

  ☐ Decide on your best sales method and explain how you'll make it happen.

  ☐ Evaluate what advertising mediums — television, radio, magazines, trade publications, Internet — work best for conveying your message and meeting budget goals and figures.

  ☐ Investigate which marketing promotions will be most effective for you. For example, contests, coupons, rebates, or free trials.

  ☐ Learn about public relations — news releases, trade shows, charity events — and how you can use these events in your marketing plan.

☐ Crunch some numbers and determine your marketing budget and advertising plan.

☐ Describe your primary method of sales, how you'll accept payments, accounting policies, and your system for customer purchasing patterns.

  ☐ Discuss your sales force, if any.

  ☐ Mention any sales promotional campaigns you have in the works.

Management and Organization Checklist

Management and organization are the heart and soul of your business. Without experienced, hard-working managers and a solid organizational foundation, your start-up won't have a very good chance of getting out of the starting blocks. This section of your start-up biz plan lets readers know your business is in good, capable hands and that it's well-organized and ready to run like a fine-tuned engine.

☐ Write a concise management and organization summary paragraph, highlighting all the important staff and structure considerations that will make your start-up a strong contender.

☐ If you're the only manager in the start-up, here's where you tout your skills, background, talents, and aptitude.

  ☐ Include your professional resume in this section.

☐ If you've got a management staff, then begin by listing them in a table of contents with names and titles.

    ☐ Then detail each of the key staff member's qualifications, education, experience, and references.

☐ Develop a segment on management responsibilities and duties.

    ☐ List each key manager's name and title and a brief description of his or her duties.

☐ Express your management's philosophy in a succinctly written paragraph or two.

☐ Mention any personnel incentives you'll use to help reduce turnover and recognize and reward achievement.

☐ If you're a one-person show, then an organizational structure isn't necessary. But if you've got an organizational structure with several key players, include a description of your departments, divisions, and works areas and identify the people in charge.

☐ In conclusion, write a short paragraph specifying how many employees you have, both full-time and part-time, and how many you may have during peak business seasons.

    ☐ Include a personnel plan, which is a chart of the departments by employee, function, and salary.

Operations Checklist

In the operations section of your biz plan, describe how you and your management team will run your business. Explaining how your business will be consistent indicates a higher level of employee efficiency, customer familiarity, and contentment. Operations consist of every policy and procedure that's devoted to making your biz work to establish consistency. Even if you haven't developed an operations manual, as you work through this section, you just might clarify some policy you didn't expect to — and that will be good for biz. (You don't have to write an operation manual for your business plan.)

☐ Write an operations summary to introduce your plan's readers to your way of doing business. (Usually written last, after completing the other operations segments.)

☐ Describe how your business is run through operations.

- [ ] Include a human resources policies segment (if you'll have or plan to have employees). Include info on:
    - [ ] Hiring procedures
    - [ ] New employee orientation
    - [ ] Employee training
    - [ ] Reviewing employee performance
    - [ ] Salaries and benefits
    - [ ] Any new positions that will be eventually filled

- [ ] Discuss your facility and location in terms of how they affect operational effectiveness.

    How does your overall square footage measure up?

    How is your site advantageous to your business?

    Does your lease agreement have good terms for your business?

- [ ] Examine all your company operations that help produce your product or service.
    - [ ] Evaluate how you manage, organize, and deploy your work force.
    - [ ] Discuss the various equipment you use to produce.
    - [ ] Explain how you'll improve production using technology.
    - [ ] Consider your methods of quality control.

- [ ] Describe your supply operations.
    - [ ] State the purchaser's name and title.
    - [ ] List the materials required, their sources, average cost per unit, and credit terms.
    - [ ] Describe any competitive edge you'll enjoy.

- [ ] Describe how your products or services are distributed to your customers.
    - [ ] List distributor names and titles.
    - [ ] Explain their reputations.
    - [ ] Indicate how you will pay them and how they will pay you.

- [ ] Discuss your fulfillment operation from your salespeople to customer delivery. Include:
    - [ ] Receipt of orders;

☐ Processing;

☐ Communications involved in getting ordered fulfilled;

☐ Advantages that help you fulfill orders; and

☐ Policies on rush orders, breakage control, and tracking.

☐ Describe your overall customer service policy.

☐ Show how you train employees and monitor their consistency.

☐ Explain your inventory control policy.

☐ Mention how your business implements efficiency controls.

☐ Indicate a policy of developing an annual business plan.

☐ Show how you'll be tuned in to the big picture of your company.

☐ Assign often-overlooked operational tasks to your staff, such as government regulation compliance, renewing licenses and permits, and safety compliance.

☐ Describe your cash-flow control policies and explain your money handling procedures.

Financial Pro Formas Checklist

To your plan's readers, this section is the most critical for assessing just how much dollars and sense your business makes. Even though these financial papers are "pro forma" or financial projections, they hold the key for many reviewers. Work closely with your accountant and calculator to make these statements work well for your start-up.

☐ Write a financial summary that highlights your key assumptions; break-even point; what you expect to do the first three or five years; and peak performances.

☐ Write a segment on the important assumptions you'll make for developing your financial material for the first three or five years of business. Assumptions to include, but aren't limited to, are:

☐ Market share

☐ Average monthly sales

☐ Cash sales

☐ Cost of sales

☐ Payroll taxes and benefits

☐ Present your company's opening balance sheet with a date that corresponds to the start of the business plan.

☐ Include a complete one-year and three-year or five-year pro forma income statement.

☐ Calculate and include your break-even analysis.

☐ Determine your pro form cash-flow statement and present it in this section as well.

☐ Include a first-year pro forma balance sheet showing your financial worth at the end of each quarter, and your three- or five-year pro forma balance sheet using year-end annual numbers.

☐ Consult with your accountant to see which business ratios you should include here. A sampling of the more popular ratios include:

  ☐ Quick ratio

  ☐ Current ratio

  ☐ Debt-to-equity ratio

  ☐ Gross profit margin

Financial Requirement Checklist

The last section in your start-up biz plan is reserved for your financial request. It expands the financial requirement you introduced in your executive summary and details the amount and type of financial assistance you're trying to obtain.

☐ Write your financial requirement summary request, after determining all the other segments for this section.

☐ Write a loan request summary paragraph. Have it answer the following:

How much money do you need?

What do you plan to use it for?

How can the money improve your business?

How are you going to pay it back?

What's your back-up plan?

☐ In a brief paragraph, describe your total start-up costs and explain major items or anything that's not easily identifiable.

☐ Next, indicate the funds you've raised so far, with a breakdown of individual amounts from different sources.

- [ ] Then, show the amount needed, listing the anticipated source and pay-back. (Amount needed should be the difference between total start-up costs and amount raised.)

- [ ] Compile a loan request proposal or investment offering, complete with a table showing all start-up costs, both hard and soft; terms requested; any remarks; and your available collateral.

- [ ] In your potential risks segment use a table or narrative summary to describe at least three major risks that you foresee for your business.

  - [ ] Offer reasons for how you'll be able to overcome and offset these risks.

- [ ] Include an exit option. (See Glossary.)

Business Plan Exhibits Checklist

Most supporting information is located in its respective sections; however, some documents are either too big or inappropriate for a particular section. But because they are still vital to the plan, group these documents in the exhibits section. It's preferable to keep your exhibits section much shorter than your entire plan's length.

- [ ] Ensure the exhibits are easy to find by starting with a table of contents of the exhibits.

  - [ ] Feature titled tabs for each exhibit for quick reference.

  - [ ] Use the same layout and format as you did for your plan's table of contents.

- [ ] Determine which documents and supporting paperwork will be included in your business plan exhibits. Examples that might apply can include:

  - [ ] Marketing materials

  - [ ] Manufacturing materials

  - [ ] Legal documents

  - [ ] Facility documentation

  - [ ] Business references

- [ ] Avoid including materials that introduce information not discussed in the business plan.

Strategies and Tips

Writing a business plan takes time and energy, but what you learn about yourself and your business is worth all the effort. Not only will you increase your odds of finding the dollars you need to get started, you'll be in stronger shape to deal with any pitfalls your business is likely to encounter. A start-up business plan creates forward thinking, planning, and troubleshooting. Here are a few bonus tips from *The Rule Book of Business Plans for Startups* for making your business plan process a little smoother.

- Take advantage of the Internet whenever possible for business plan research. It's fast, convenient, and a time-saver.

- Always include a cover letter with your business plan because it may get passed on to other staff members who won't know about your venture. So write your cover letter as though the reader knows nothing about you or your business to cover all your bases.

- The U.S. Census Bureau has numerous publications available to the public regarding economic and business ratios and rates. Take full advantage of their services and information. Refer to Appendix D's marketing sites section for its web site.

- The Service Corps of Retired Executives (SCORE) is a wonderful resource for business plan consulting. Just go to their web site (See Appendix D.) and ask about their free consulting services. SCORE is affiliated with the U.S. Small Business Administration.

- Once you've completed your start-up business plan, hire a professional proofreader or editor to review it for punctuation, grammatical, or organizational errors.

- Like cause and effect, use your business plan findings to develop your opportunities.

- To really know your customers, learn not only who they are, but what they want.

- Impress prospective investors with well-defined long-term goals. (Most start-ups skip over this aspect of planning and investors give this section serious review.)

- Understand your market findings. If your products or services won't have the market to keep it afloat, it won't matter how hard you work to succeed. Know your market!

- Don't feel like you have to balance the material in your business plan. Instead, place more emphasis on your strong points and talk up those features most important to your business.

Helpful Resources

Here are some business resources that will help you compile and write your business plan. For more of the same, you can refer to the appendices in the back of the book for info on SBDCs, biz magazines and other publications, and online resources for small business.

ABCs of Borrowing
U.S. Small Business Administration
(800) 827-5722

This handy publication helps explain borrowing fundamentals in a concise, easy-to-read format.

The Business Plan for Home-Based Businesses
U.S. Small Business Administration
(800) 827-5722

If you're convinced that a profitable home business is attainable, this publication will provide a step-by-step guide to developing a business plan.

Current Industrial Reports (CIRs)
Economic Censuses
County Business Patterns
U.S. Bureau of the Census
(301) 457-4608

CIRs provide info on production, shipping, inventories, consumption, and the number of firms manufacturing each product. The *Economic Censuses* report on monthly sales figures and trends for various industries. The *County Business Patterns* help evaluate the performance and trends of your industry in your target location.

Dialog
(800) 3-DIALOG

Dialog, an on-line database, incorporates more than 300 different databases, including Dun & Bradstreet and Standard & Poor's. Dialog also contains Findex, which catalogs and describes industry and market research studies that are available commercially.

The New Product Development Planner
American Management Association (AMA)
1 (888) 281-5092

This book guides you through every stage of the development process and takes you through every issue and consideration to increase your chances for success.

Venture Capital Primer
U.S. Small Business Administration
(800) 827-5722

This publication highlights what venture capital resources are available, plus it explains how to develop a proposal for obtaining these funds.

Helpful Resources from The Oasis Press

The Oasis Press — The Leading Publisher of Small Business Information publishes several books that will assist you in writing your business plan. You can order these books from your local bookstore, or call the company directly at:

The Oasis Press
(800) 228-2275

businessplan.com

Nope, this isn't a web site — this book's on the cutting edge with its advice on how to gather and research info from the Internet and write a knock-out business plan.

Financing Your Small Business

Identify, approach, attract, and manage sources of financing with the tricks and techniques outlined by a savvy money manager.

Funding High-Tech Ventures

Discover an insider's proven strategies for getting your state-of-the-art biz idea off the starting line with funding, product development, and marketing.

Know Your Market: How to Do Low-Cost Market Research

Find out where to go and how to get the market research info you need with this do-it-yourself guide.

Insider's Guide to Small Business Loans

Get some tips on simplifying the loan process, preparing the loan application, and dealing with the Small Business Administration.

Marketing for the New Millennium

One step above the usual how-to marketing books, this forward-looking book discusses combining marketing techniques and angles for the Year 2000 and beyond.

Marketing Mastery: Your Seven Step Guide to Success

Get your product or service off the ground and running with this beginner's look and trek through marketing.

Navigating the Marketplace: Growth Strategies for Your Business

Design your biz to target different types of customers and learn to recognize solid marketing strategies and techniques to make sure you get the most out of your marketing efforts.

Power Marketing for Small Business

A great marketing resource for the start-up biz owner — a friendly, basic look at the world of marketing and advertising.

The Rule Book of Business Plans for Startups

A business plan book just for start-ups! Learn the unique "rules" for structuring, compiling, and writing your start-up business plan so you get the dollars you need. Along the way, discover your strengths and weaknesses and use your plan to overcome potential pitfalls.

The Small Business Insider's Guide to Bankers

A great source for ways to meet the right banker and get the funding you need from them. Learn what they're looking for and what you need to bring to make it all happen.

SmartStart Your (State) Business series

A unique start-up business guide for small business owners because of its one-stop, federal and state-specific info. It's all you need to know to start a business in your state. A must-have biz resource!

Notes

Plan of Action for a Business Plan

Your company will write a business plan: ☐ Yes ☐ No

Use this planning tool to organize and prioritize the activities in this chapter that you've checked off. Don't feel you have to list all the activities you've checked off. Simply start with the top ten most important ones and go from there, or do whatever is easiest for you. Make plenty of copies of this cut-out worksheet for your planning and organizing activities for this chapter.

Action to be Taken	Begin Date	Who	Deadline

Plan of Action (continued)

Action to be Taken	Begin Date	Who	Deadline

Chapter 8

Buying a Business or Franchise

Introduction

Perhaps starting a business from the ground up isn't what you want to do, and you're more interested in the opportunities that lie with buying an existing business or franchise operation. If this is the case, this chapter will give you a general overview of what to do and what to investigate when purchasing an existing business or franchise.

Buying a business or franchise is an involved process and one that demands you retain the services of a qualified attorney and accountant. By reading this chapter, you'll have a better idea of what to ask your advisers and what they should include in their investigations. As a general guide, try to keep these essential questions in mind when reviewing any business that is for sale:

- Can you earn a living from the business?
- Can you manage the business yourself?
- Can you enjoy the business?
- Can you afford to buy the business?

Be honest and candid in your answers to these questions, and if you answer "yes" to each of them, then you can proceed with your investigation of the potential business or franchise. Be sure you have covered all your bases! By buying a business the right way, you can jump out ahead in the business game, but by not doing it right, you could drop out of the game completely.

First Aid for Buying a Business or Franchise

 To avoid dropping out of the game completely, you can purchase a couple of book sources to help you stay on track. One such source is *The Secrets to Buying and Selling a Business* by Ira N. Nottonson. This handy book prepares a business buyer or seller for negotiations that will achieve win-win results when purchasing or selling a business.

Another book is *Franchise Bible: How to Buy a Franchise or Franchise Your Own Business*, written by Erwin Keup. This book is a comprehensive guide that explains in detail what the franchise system entails and the benefits it offers. The book contains an actual offering circular to familiarize you with the terms and considerations franchisees face. You can order these books directly from the publisher or purchase them from a local bookstore.

Franchise Bible
The Secrets to Buying and Selling a Small Business
The Oasis Press
(800) 228-2275

Buying a Business

The idea of having an established customer base and receiving an income the first month after taking ownership of an existing business can make the decision to purchase an existing business over starting one from scratch very appealing. In fact, the cost of buying an existing business is usually comparable to the investment ultimately required in starting a new business. Indeed, many of the rigors and risks of starting from scratch are nonexistent with the successful purchase of an existing business; however, the purchasing process isn't one to be taken lightly.

For you to enjoy the advantages of owning an established business, be well informed on how to:

- Properly research the business and the appropriate trade or industry;
- Consider the financial variables and growth potential of the business by examining the history and progress of its growth;
- Value the assets of the business and be careful to note potential obsolescence of inventory and equipment;

- Work with a potential partner or investor to ensure stability and control, being particularly careful to understand whether this person's goals and aspirations are consistent with your own; and

- Negotiate the sale to ensure you will get what you pay for and protect against misrepresentations.

In addition, you'll also need to know about the closing of the sale and various tax and other legal considerations. To help you get an idea of what's involved in the purchasing process, the checklists in this section are designed to highlight important purchasing factors.

Before entering into negotiations with a seller, commit yourself to the time and energy it'll take to become familiar with purchasing terminology, procedures, and legal requirements. To help ensure your success in this particular aspect of the business game, gather a strong team of professionals, attend any related seminars in your area, and purchase helpful books on the subject.

Research Checklist

Before you even begin to do any prepurchase research, seriously consider what type of business best fits your particular skills and talents. Know your strengths and weaknesses. Remember that nearly all businesses today need managers and owners with strong selling skills. In addition, understand your level of commitment to your future business and make sure your family is supportive and informed. With a review of these personal factors, you'll then be better prepared to target specific businesses for research. Use this checklist for every business you consider purchasing.

☐ Develop your research questions so they're specific and direct.

 Did the industry or trade grow in size last year?

How much is it expected to grow in the next year?

What products or services are in greatest demand? And by whom?

What problems do suppliers have providing products and a consistent price?

☐ Ask an existing competitor (or franchisee) for a general description of what the business and particular industry entails.

☐ Consult with your business consultant, attorney, and accountant to get their opinions on the business.

☐ Read trade magazines to inform yourself of the latest technology, trends, and innovations in the industry.

☐ Talk to the business' vendors and suppliers so you get a better view of the industry.

☐ Review the answers to your research questions and reevaluate them to glean even more information.

☐ Find out why the owner wants to sell the business.

> Is any portion of the inventory or equipment becoming obsolete?
> Does the owner know of a new competitor coming to the area?
> Is the business unable to support the owner?
> Is the owner simply wanting to retire?

☐ Consider your funding resources and the business' ability to service debt and provide you with an income.

> Will you simply need to make enough to keep the business going and support your family?
> Or, must the business help pay back the money you borrowed to buy the business?

☐ Examine and read the sales materials carefully.

☐ Do a historical analysis of the business.

☐ Get a feeling for the business' impact on its existing customer base.

☐ Talk with current customers, employees, and suppliers of the business to get feedback on the business and its product or service.

☐ Investigate whether there's a loyalty factor that will cause a degradation of the customer base after the sale.

☐ Visit the prospective business in person to get a first-hand feel and view of the facilities, the traffic patterns, the surrounding area, the population mix, and the neighborhood.

☐ Determine how the business' reputation will be affected if you take over the business.

☐ Ask yourself why you think you can make the business even better, if it's a profitable business. If it's an unprofitable business, ask yourself why and how you would do a better job.

Financial Considerations Checklist

The first decision you face as you consider buying a business is how to finance it. Three essential factors are involved in that decision: your cash return, your level of risk, and your financing method. These factors are briefly highlighted in the checklist below. Become familiar with these terms and make sure your accountant helps you evaluate them when considering any potential business purchase.

At this point, work with the seller in early negotiations to get access to the records and documents that'll allow you to recognize the financial responsibilities of the business, both in the short term and the long term.

The success of negotiations depends in great part on the relationship established between the parties at the beginning of the buying and selling process. So if you can establish trust early on, you'll find the process will go much smoother.

☐ Compare the return your cash investment will yield in the existing business with the return it receives in its current stocks, mutual funds, or savings accounts.

☐ Obtain all previous tax returns, bank deposit records, and other financial records of the business to track its financial health and history.

    ☐ Examine accounts receivables and collection policies.

    ☐ Request the previous three years' profit and loss statements, balance sheets, and cash-flow analyses.

    ☐ Review the business' financial history via the profit and loss statements and balance sheets.

☐ Recast the previous profit and loss statement to see what your profit would be if you bought the business.

☐ Thoroughly investigate the business' reputation and other intangible factors that might have an impact on its future.

☐ Determine the level of risk involved with the investment.

    What are the financial percentages involved?

    Is there any possibility that the equipment or inventory may become obsolete?

    Does the business' success depend on the present owner's ability to sell, or is it because of her personal contact with key customers?

    Is the location the most vital part of the business?

☐ Determine how you'll finance your business purchase.

    Will you have a cash-in-full purchase, or will you need a down payment and owner financing?

    What funding resources do you need and possess?

    What purchase alternatives are available, such as interest rate or length of purchase money promissory note, that might adjust the price and make the sale possible?

Valuing Assets Checklist

Once you have done as much general, prepurchase research as possible, and evaluated your financial considerations, you'll want to look more specifically at the selling price. An existing business offers many types of assets, and each asset's value will eventually be figured into the selling price in one way or another.

To determine the value of the asset variables, do some research on your own; consult appraisers, accountants, or attorneys; and request specific information from your seller. The checklist below is designed to help you value a business' assets so you can decide whether to proceed further into negotiations.

☐ Determine whether a business' equipment is outdated, obsolete, or state-of-the-art.

    ☐ If outdated or obsolete, calculate how much it'll cost to update or replace the equipment to ensure the business' competitive edge and use this as a negotiating point for a lower price.

☐ Investigate whether the business' particular industry is expecting any technological innovations with equipment that may affect its operations.

☐ Check with the appropriate state or local authorities involved in maintaining ownership records and assure that there's not a lien or an encumbrance on the equipment.

☐ Review equipment maintenance records and status of company warranties.

☐ Personally evaluate the inventory of the business.

    Is the inventory's volume currently too high or too low? Is it obsolete or valuable?

    What dollar amount are you willing to pay for it as part of the purchase price?

☐ Make sure the seller actually owns the inventory, has paid for it, and has not pledged or otherwise used it for security.

☐ Ask if any real estate is involved with the purchase. If so, then have a separate analysis of the real estate done by a professional appraiser.

    What is the fair market value of the real estate?

    What is the value of the property without the business as a tenant?

    Will the property be worth more as time goes on?

    Is the property free and clear of all liens or encumbrances?

☐ Understand all the terms and conditions of the lease, if applicable.

☐ If a building is for sale, along with the business, determine if it is in good condition and have its value appraised.

> Is asbestos present in the building?
>
> Is there an environmental clean-up problem involved at the property?
>
> Does it need a new roof?
>
> What are the annual maintenance costs and repairs?

☐ Consider the value of the business' highly qualified employees and their relationships to the business' existing customer base.

☐ Evaluate the effectiveness and value of the business' location.

☐ Be prepared to pay for the benefit of a business that has a recognizable logo, an established trade name, or a favorable reputation.

☐ Determine the value of a business' computer hardware and software to make sure you're paying for an effective, efficient system.

☐ Determine if the absence or presence of competition for the business is desirable or not, and take that into consideration when assessing the selling price.

Investor or Partner Checklist

Some business sales can occur in one simple transaction with the buyer taking over the business right away and doing so on her own; however, many other business sales require the seller to stay on as a paid consultant, investor, or partner. Not all partners or investors are former owners, though such an arrangement is one way to creatively finance a sale. Often, buyers need the participation of other people for money, guidance, or actual labor. If you're considering taking on an investor or partner or becoming one yourself, the checklist below will alert you to some of the issues related to sharing control of your business. As always, consult an attorney and accountant before you finalize any investor or partnership deal.

☐ Be aware that by accepting investment capital, you're giving up a degree of control over your business.

☐ Know what your investor's or partner's goals are.

> Are those goals consistent with your goals?
>
> Will your business venture satisfy your investor's or partner's goals?
>
> Do you think that short-term thinking by the investors to protect their investment might subvert your long-term goals?

☐ Consider a realistic timetable with the investor or partner for when the business will be able to pay back the investment, give a return on the investment, or buy out the partner, if that's your intent.

☐ Discuss the legal form of doing business, such as a partnership or corporation, with your partners or investors.

☐ Understand what joint and several liability is. See the Glossary.

☐ Determine if an employee or paid consultant can fill your need for expertise, rather than an investor or partner, should you only need a partner for his personal knowledge and experience in your type of business.

☐ Work out a comfortable buyout arrangement between you and your partners for when you choose to dissolve the partnership.

Negotiating Price Checklist

By the time you are ready to begin pricing negotiations, you have already had some initial contact with the seller. During this time, you have hopefully created an environment of trust and the seller realizes you are a serious, prospective buyer. The main factor that will affect the price negotiations will be how you pay for the business — cash-in-full or with a down payment and financing. You will need your accountant to help you with this part of the negotiations process. The checklist below gives you an idea of what to include in your price negotiations.

☐ Decide if you'll do an all-cash deal or make a down payment with an owner-carry contract.

    ☐ If an all-cash deal, expect a bigger concession in the selling price.

    ☐ If a down payment deal, determine the amount of your initial down payment, negotiate the length of the note, and negotiate the interest rate.

    ☐ Once the down payment, length of note, and interest rate have been negotiated, you should be able to discuss a reasonable selling price.

☐ Remember the operating profit of the business is the key to creating a selling price, for example, a higher operating profit allows a seller to ask a higher price.

☐ Push for an allocation of the purchase price to specific assets in the sales agreement. Discuss the advantages of doing this with your accountant.

    ☐ Seek to maximize the amounts allocable to depreciable assets and any noncompetition covenant.

    ☐ Seek to minimize allocations to goodwill or land purchased.

☐ Look for hidden liabilities against the business and make sure they are taken care of in the sales agreement. For instance:

> Are there any pending lawsuits?
>
> Do any current employees have accrued vacation coming to them?
>
> Do any employees have any close relationships with any large, existing customers?
>
> Are there any unfunded pension plan liabilities?
>
> What about any potential exposure to environmental clean-up costs?

Closing the Transaction Checklist

Once you've completed negotiations and are satisfied with the results, you'll be ready to close the deal. To close a deal, you'll need to do several activities, some of which are required legally. These requirements, as well as other activities, are listed in the checklist below.

☐ Retain an attorney to participate in drawing up the sales agreement.

☐ Comply with any bulk sale laws in your state by checking with the secretary of state's office for details. See definition for bulk sale laws in the Glossary.

☐ Be sure the acquired property is not subject to any recorded security interests or other liens beyond those disclosed by the seller. To do this, have your attorney conduct a thorough search of the appropriate offices.

☐ Have the seller obtain and furnish you with a certificate stating that sales and use taxes and unemployment taxes have been paid.

☐ Seek to hold back part of the purchase price as security to reimburse you for any misrepresentations as to assets or liabilities by the seller.

☐ Make provisions for acquiring customer mailing lists or any other collateral assets on which the continuity of the business may depend.

☐ Prepare *Form 8594, Asset Acquisition Statement*, and file it with the IRS once the deal is closed.

☐ Check with your state government to ensure you complete any state requirements regarding the purchase of a business, such as bulk sales laws or notification of transfer of ownership.

Other Tax and Legal Considerations Checklist

Despite the activities listed above, there are some other items to consider when thinking about purchasing a business. This checklist attempts to compile a few of these miscellaneous, yet important items so you and your advisers don't forget them.

☐ Determine whether the sale of the business will result in a sales tax liability with respect to part or all of the purchase price.

☐ If buying a corporation that hasn't paid income taxes because of carry-overs of net operating losses, be aware you may be able to use only a small portion of those carryovers to shelter the income of the business once you become the owner.

☐ Check the seller's workers' compensation insurance rate to see how your rate will be assessed.

    ☐ Determine if you can succeed to the seller's rate or if you'll receive a new one.

☐ Check the seller's experience tax rating for unemployment tax purposes, and if it's better than the tax rating you'd receive as a new employer, then see if you can succeed to that favorable rating.

    ☐ Contact your state's employment service department for more information on succeeding to experience tax ratings.

☐ Understand your obligations under the Foreign Investment in Real Property Tax Act (FIRPTA) if you purchase real estate from a "foreign person."

    ☐ Contact the IRS for more information on FIRPTA.

☐ Hire a licensed expert to perform due-diligence environmental testing of the property. This is especially important if the business handles or produces hazardous wastes. The term, due-diligence, is defined in the Glossary.

    ☐ Inspect the neighboring properties, if possible.

    ☐ Pay close attention to property boundaries. Even if the waste comes from a neighboring property, you'll be liable for any waste found on your property.

☐ Negotiate with the owners of any adjoining empty lots to control and account for all dumping there.

☐ Ask the current owner if he has had any problems with sick building syndrome. See the Glossary.

☐ Determine if underground tanks are present on the property. If so, consider:

What were they used for?

What is the viable lifetime of the tanks?

Is there evidence of contamination or damage to the ground, groundwater, flora, or fauna?

Will you have to fill or remove the tanks?

☐ Consult your state environmental department to determine which requirements apply to the business you're buying.

☐ Determine if operating licenses or leases can be transferred or if you'll need to apply for new ones.

☐ See if you'll be able to transfer intangible property rights, such as patents, trademarks, or copyrights.

☐ Have your attorney review all provisions of key contracts, leases, or any other legal arrangements that have a significant effect on the business.

Buying a Franchise

Buying a franchise is different than buying an existing business because of the unique relationship that exists between the franchisor and franchisee. In a franchise relationship, you can enjoy less risk, more management support, more profits, additional financing, and numerous advertising benefits. On the other hand, you pay fees, royalties, and down payments, plus you don't have as much control or flexibility in running the business.

Regardless, franchising is a very common way to start a new business in today's business world, and if you're still considering ways to start your business, the information in this section may prove helpful. Review the checklist in this section and the Helpful Resources at the end of this chapter for more on how to investigate and buy a franchise. Keep in mind that the process of buying a franchise demands careful investigation and professional assistance from attorneys and accountants.

Buying a Franchise Checklist

The checklist below is a general overview of what to think about when considering buying a franchise. If you're seriously considering a franchise as your new business, you may find the book, *Franchise Bible*, very helpful.

☐ List the franchises that most interest you.

_____

_____

_____

_____

_____

_____

☐ Research the names and addresses of these franchises. See this chapter's Helpful Resources for hints on where to look for franchise listings.

☐ Write to each of the franchise headquarters and request a copy of its uniform franchise offering circular.

    ☐ Investigate what an offering circular should contain.

☐ Evaluate each franchise by reviewing its circular and by interviewing existing franchisees, failed franchisees, suppliers, and the franchisor.

☐ Make a final selection and move towards negotiating a contract.

☐ Hire an experienced franchise attorney, who's also familiar with the FTC franchise law that became effective in January 1995, to review disclosure statements and help you with any negotiations.

☐ Review the contract and have a clear idea of what should be included in the document. Consider:

What are the initial costs and fees of the franchise?

Where will the location of the franchise be and will other franchisees be allowed in the same area?

Who controls hours and prices?

What kind of training will you receive as a franchisee?

How will any co-op advertising work?

What kind of financing is available through the franchisor?

What items must you purchase from the franchisor, and do you have the option to buy them locally, if they are cheaper?

☐ Investigate the use of the franchisor's trademarks and service marks.

Is the trademark well-known?

What rights do you have as a franchisee for use of these marks?

Strategies and Tips

As a prospective buyer of an existing business or as a prospective franchisee, you need to gain as much information and knowledge as you can about the buying process, including negotiations and contract writing. Since this can be a highly complicated process, be sure to retain the services of an experienced attorney and review the tips and helpful resources mentioned below.

- Business brokers and realtors can be excellent sources for finding a business that's for sale. You can also look for ads in local newspapers, or ask your lawyer or accountant.

- An attorney and accountant are necessary members of your buying team. Get the team together early in the process.

- Doing research and asking questions may be embarrassing, time-consuming, and tedious, but they're absolutely necessary to ensure you make the right decision.

- Your funding resources must be equal to the business' financial demands. No amount of skill or commitment will make a business a success without the necessary working capital.

- A business is composed of many parts. Make sure you understand what each part represents and how it contributes to the success of the business.

- A business' financial statements provide the history of the business and insight into its current value and future growth. Go over the profit and loss statement, balance sheet, cash-flow analysis, and general ledger carefully with your professional advisers.

- Don't let your emotions lead you toward an investment that doesn't utilize your particular talents and experience. It can be fun, but it can also be dangerous.

- Consider a franchise only if it presents more of an opportunity than you could provide for yourself.

- When dealing with franchising, be wary of any franchise opportunity touting $1,000–3,000 starter kits. This may be too good to be true.

- Try to avoid pyramid schemes in franchising where you buy an area franchise and subfranchise to others.

- If you're not willing to play by the franchisor's rules, then don't buy a franchise. You'd be better off to start your own business or buy an existing one.

- Have your attorney and accountant explain all the elements that constitute your relationship with the franchise company. Know your obligations and prerogatives.
- A good place to check out existing businesses and franchises is the Better Business Bureau. Make this step a part of your initial investigation.

Helpful Resources

Here are some business resources that will help you buy an existing business or a franchise. For more of the same, you can refer to the appendices in the back of the book for info on SBDCs, biz magazines and other publications, and online resources for small business.

American Franchisee Association (AFA)
(800) 334-4AFA

This group aims to represent and educate franchisees and protect their economic investments. A good group for anyone interested in joining the world of franchising.

Buying Your First Franchise
Crisp Publications
(800) 442-7477

This book will help you first-time buyers make the decisions about which franchise to buy, how to finance it, and how to make it succeed.

Franchise Annual Directory
Info Franchise News
(716) 754-4669

Includes more than 4,000 listings of franchise opportunities, plus contact info, fees, and brief descriptions.

Franchise Opportunities Handbook
U.S. Government Printing Office
(202) 512-0000

Call for the latest edition of this annual compilation of existing U.S. franchises. It may help you find an opportunity to start your own biz.

Franchising Magazine
Linfield, Australia
(02) 9880 7777

Get this monthly magazine that focuses on franchisees. You'll get tips for self-analyses, where to go for advice, test developments, and much more!

International Franchise Association
(202) 628-8000

This association publishes several titles on franchise topics and is a savvy resource for anyone interested in franchising opportunities and operations.

Helpful Resources from The Oasis Press

The Oasis Press — The Leading Publisher of Small Business Information publishes several books that will assist you in your quest for buying an existing business or a franchise. You can order these books from your local bookstore, or call the company directly at:

The Oasis Press
(800) 228-2275

Franchise Bible: How to Buy a Franchise or Franchise Your Own Business

A virtual one-stop resource for what you'll need to know to buy that franchise you've been dreaming of. This book will save time and dollars and provide you with info on franchising trends, topics, and documents to get you in the franchise game.

The Franchise Redbook

Get the scoop on hundreds of franchisors, as well as the industry itself.

No Money Down Financing for Franchising

Find out how to get financing for your franchise opportunity with this three-part guide on making a franchise acquisition.

The Secrets to Buying and Selling a Business

A solid source for helping you learn about the purchasing process from start to finish. Plus tips for recognizing when a sale's a winner or a loser.

SmartStart Your (State) Business series

A unique start-up guide for small business owners because of its one-stop, federal and state-specific info. It's all you need to know to start a business in your state. A must-have biz resource!

What's It Worth? A Guide to Valuing a Business

Identify a golden business opportunity and calculate what price to pay. Learn to appraise small businesses; place value on assets, customer base, and goodwill; and interpret income and retained earnings.

Notes

_____

_____

_____

_____

_____

_____

_____

_____

_____

_____

_____

_____

_____

_____

_____

_____

_____

_____

_____

_____

_____

_____

_____

_____

_____

_____

_____

_____

Plan of Action for Buying a Business or Franchise

My company will be buying:
☐ An existing business   ☐ A franchise

Use this planning tool to organize and prioritize the activities in this chapter that you've checked off. Don't feel you have to list all the activities you've checked off. Simply start with the top ten most important ones and go from there, or do whatever is easiest for you. Make plenty of copies of this cut-out worksheet for your planning and organizing activities for this chapter.

Action to be Taken	Begin Date	Who	Deadline

Plan of Action (continued)

Action to be Taken	Begin Date	Who	Deadline

Glossary

Accounts receivable financing. Accounts receivables represent the money owed to a business from credit sales to its customers. Next to cash, receivables are the most liquid of any firm's assets and they can be converted to cash within a short period of time. These qualities make receivables a desirable asset for any firm to hold, and for the same reason, often make desirable collateral for a loan.

Affirmative action program. An affirmative action program is a plan for recruiting, hiring, training, and promoting minorities in industries where their numbers are low. Your business is probably not required to have such a program, unless you have certain federal government contracts.

Balance sheet. The balance sheet offers an overview of a firm's sources and amounts of financing, and how these funds have been used. This is an important document when making business decisions regarding financing.

Bond insurance. Bonds are a form of insurance that allow a third party to be guaranteed performance or compensated for nonperformance of a service a business or individual may perform. It's not uncommon for a bond to be required before someone will award you a contract. There are two types of bonds: 1) fidelity bonds are used to guarantee honest performance of employees; and 2) surety bonds are posted to guarantee the performance of a company.

Browser. Software program that allows a user to navigate and view files on the Internet's World Wide Web.

Bulk sale law. When a business sells all or substantially all of its assets or enters into a major transaction that is not part of its ordinary business activities, the bulk sales law applies. The purpose of this law is to protect the rights of creditors, such as suppliers and others, who have advanced goods or money to a business and have not yet been paid; however, in recent years, these laws have been repealed in many states because of their complexity. Check to see if your state has repealed its bulk sale law.

Buying cycle. This is the time span from when a prospect becomes aware of a product or service to when he purchases it. Depending on the nature and cost of the product or service, the cycle could be days, weeks, or years.

Bylaws. The bylaws are the rules and procedures that govern a corporation. Such things as director and shareholder meetings and procedures are described in the bylaws. In the event of a conflict between the articles of incorporation and the bylaws, the articles control. Bylaws can't be inconsistent with a state's business corporation act.

Cash-flow projection. The cash-flow projection measures the cash impact of a firm's operating, investing, and financing activities over a given time period. This statement effectively combines balance sheet and income statement data to provide a summary of the sources of cash available to a business and how this cash was used. These variables are by far the most important indicators of a firm's financial health.

Cogeneration. Using the same fuel source to produce electricity and a useful heat energy at the same time is referred to as cogeneration.

Commercial bank. A commercial bank is a financial institution that obtains most of its working capital by accepting deposits from its customers. Depositors' funds are then used to conduct the bank's primary business of making loans and investments.

Commercial finance company. A commercial finance company is a lending institution that makes only secured short- and long-term loans to businesses. They offer no checking or savings account services. They are the business world's counterpart to consumer finance companies.

Cooperative or co-op advertising. Cooperative advertising is a method of sharing advertising costs with noncompetitive companies that target the same market as you do. It can help you generate more sales for less money.

Corporation. A corporation is a more complicated form of doing business because it's considered a distinct legal entity and has a legal status or existence separate from the owner or incorporator. One of the main advantages to incorporating is that you're not personally liable for corporation debts, as long as you comply with necessary corporate formalities. It's more expensive and complicated to incorporate and the help of an attorney is recommended.

Database (or relationship) marketing. Database marketing uses a database to specifically target and profile customers better, and it also penetrates the market through telemarketing or direct mail contacts. This type of marketing promotes regularly scheduled contacts and strong customer service. In other words, you develop strong relationships with customers so you can increase sales and reduce costs.

Daylighting. Daylighting uses the sun to light work areas via skylights and windows.

Debt financing. Debt financing represents the funds provided by creditors under a legally binding, contractual agreement. The contract obligates the borrower or debtor to repay the money or credit advanced, plus stipulated interest, at some designated future date, and to honor all other specified provisions or restrictions.

Demographics. The identification of common characteristics of a population — especially those of age, sex, income, and education — that allows you to determine to whom you should address your advertising message.

Due-diligence. This is proof or documentation that you have diligently inspected the property you are buying and found no environmental problems.

Employee handbook. An employee handbook includes your company's basic rules and regulations, usually only two to three pages in length. This is followed by information such as company history, procedures, benefits, and employee performance guidelines. Typically, an employee handbook is created from a company's policy and personnel manual, which consists of written policies and guidelines for both management and employees. In short, the employee handbook is a simplified version of the company's manual.

Equity financing. Equity financing is raised by selling a portion of a firm's ownership interest to an outsider of the business.

Executive summary. A business plan's executive summary gives the reader a chance to quickly understand your basic business concept. It helps the reader decide whether to commit more time to reading the entire plan.

Exit option. An exit option or strategy is included in your business plan for your investors' sake. It outlines how investors can opt out of your business at some future point. The most appealing option for them is a buy-out; however, you have several other options to explore.

Factoring company or house. A factoring company (or factor) pays cash for accounts receivables so that you can get use of your cash without waiting for 30, 60, or 90 days, depending on your credit terms. However, you'll have to discount the receivables and may have to take back any bad accounts. Not all companies use factors, and factors may not take your accounts.

Fictitious business name. An assumed or fictitious business name is any name used in the course of business that does not include the full legal name of all the owners of the business. If your business goes by any name other than your own real name, your business is operating under a fictitious name.

Floor plan financing. Floor plan financing occurs when a retail operation sells large ticket items, such as appliances, trailers, boats, and cars. To finance each item's purchase, the bank will only charge interest payments on the item until it's sold. Once it's sold, then the retailer pays off the principal amount of the item.

Freight forwarder. A freight forwarder is an independent warehouser and shipper who handles domestic and international shipments for manufacturers who don't have the means to deliver everywhere they need to. The manufacturer pays the freight forwarder for this service.

Greywater. This is water that has already been used for nontoxic purposes, such as washing, food rinsing, or cooling.

Income statement. The income statement is a summary of the sales revenues earned in a given period and the expenses that were incurred in earning that revenue.

Independent contractor. An independent contractor is an individual who contracts her services out to a number of companies for compensation. This person's not considered an employee of the company, thus allowing the company to save on personnel paperwork and payroll taxes.

Joint and several liability. In a general partnership, joint and several liability makes any individual partner 100 percent responsible for any partnership obligation, regardless of whether that partner was solely or only partially responsible for the creation of the debt.

Leasing company. An independent leasing company provides your business with employees and takes care of all personnel functions from hiring to firing.

Limited liability company. A limited liability company (LLC) isn't a corporation or partnership, yet it combines the corporate characteristic of limited liability for owners with partnership-type taxation. Advantages of selecting LLC status include pass-through tax treatment, limited liability, and active management participation.

Line of credit. If you have seasonal or cyclical needs for cash, a line of credit may work for you. You may need to pay off the line for a 30-day period each twelve months, just to show that you don't need the loan for long-term financing. See what conditions your bank places on this type of borrowing.

Low-cost/no-cost measures. These are environment-friendly actions that require little expenditure to implement, such as providing reusable cups for your employees, or require no expenditure at all, such as reusing inter-office envelopes.

Management information system (MIS). An MIS is a systematic way of collecting, organizing, and distributing information to management in a summarized form to help them in planning, controlling, and making decisions about a company.

Market segment. A market segment is any group of consumers who have the same reaction to a given marketing stimulus. To be economically feasible, a market segment must be reachable through some means of communication, and it must be large enough to warrant a seller's effort.

Marketing plan. This plan outlines how to successfully penetrate, capture, and maintain desired positions in identified markets. In addition, it defines the goals, principles, and methods that determine a company's future.

Media kits. A media kit is usually provided by a particular advertising medium and contains the kind of information you need to evaluate its advertising value. The media kit usually contains demographic and psychographic data of the medium audience, third-party circulation audits, and ad rates.

Media mix. Media mix is the combination of various communication instruments or channels — such as newspaper, video tape, magazines, or television — that effectively reach your target market. Using a combination of media can help you appear more credible and establish repetition of your message faster than using one medium alone.

News release. This document relates newsworthy information to a media source and should be written with the most vital information contained in the first paragraph. The first paragraph of a news release should answer the Five W's: who, what, where, when, and why.

Noncompetitive covenant. An agreement between the buyer and the seller, whereby the seller agrees not to compete with the buyer after the sale is complete.

Partnership. Any two or more individuals or entities who agree to contribute money, labor, property, or skill to a business and who agree to share in its profits, losses, and management are considered to have a partnership. A partnership can be organized in two different ways: as a general or as a limited partnership.

Pro forma. This is a term used to designate future cash estimates for a business rather than using data from past experience. Therefore, a pro forma income statement is an estimate of income for the number of years you project into the future. By doing projections, you can anticipate when you'll need cash and thus avoid running to the bank when you're in a financial crisis.

Psychographics. The lifestyle characteristics of a target market, such as hobbies, preferences, or social groups. These characteristics tell you what type of appeal may be most effective in reaching your prospect.

Representative or rep firms. Representative or rep firms are companies that contract with other companies to sell their products or services.

S corporation. An S corporation is a private corporation of 75 or fewer stockholders who pay personal income rather than corporate income tax on net profits. A corporation may elect to be treated as an S corporation under the Internal Revenue Code. Stringent rules exist with respect to how and when the election is made; the number and type of shareholders; and the means by which the election may be terminated.

Sales environment. The physical surroundings that set the stage so you can make your sales presentation as effectively as possible. A sales environment could be a retail location, client's office, or an outside meeting place, such as a restaurant.

Sales forecasting. This is the process of projecting your sales over a specific period of time.

Service mark. A service mark is the name used by a business to designate its service, such as Smith Legal Services or Smith Car Washes.

Sick building syndrome. This is the condition where building materials cause sickness or serious discomfort to employees.

Sole proprietorship. A sole proprietorship is a business that's owned by one person. Because there are no formal legal requirements for setting up a sole proprietorship, it's a relatively simple form to start and operate. A sole proprietor is personally liable for all business debts and must be aware of this risk and prepare for it. On the other hand, a sole proprietor can reap all the profits from the business.

Source reduction. Source reduction occurs when you reduce the amount of materials, or the quantity of a particular material, used to accomplish a specific task in your operations.

Spot. Most broadcast (television and radio) media buyers and salespeople refer to their advertisements or commercials as "spots."

Telemarketing. Telemarketing is a sales call that's made by phone. It can be used solely as an advertising method to generate interest and direct sales.

Temporary employment agencies. Temporary employment agencies specialize in "renting out" employees to fill a short-term need in a company for whatever length of time is required.

Test marketing. This is a small-scale introduction of a new product or service to test its attributes and salability. Test marketing results provide information on how the product or service must be refined to best suit the market's needs, thus providing a better opportunity for the product or service to succeed when it is finally "rolled out" on a full-scale basis.

Trade credit insurance. Trade credit insurance is probably most important where you depend on one or more companies to purchase most of your goods or services and where their nonpayment of an invoice would put you out of business.

Trademark. A trademark represents the brand name that designates a company's products, such as its car, food product, or invention. An example of a trademark would be Corvette, Fig Newton, or NordicTrack.

Trade name. A trade name designates a business, whether it's a sole proprietorship, partnership, or corporation. An example of a trade name would be Microsoft, Pepsi-Cola Company, or Nabisco.

Usenet. An original subset of the entire, vast collection of Internet newsgroups organized hierarchically by subject of interest.

Uniform franchise offering circular or FTC disclosure document. By law, the franchiser must provide this document to you: 1) at his first face-to-face personal meeting with you or the time for making disclosures regarding the terms and conditions of the sale of the franchise; 2) ten days before your making any payment to the franchiser; and 3) ten days before the signing of any contract committing you to buy the franchise, whichever occurs first.

Usury laws. Usury laws define the maximum amount of interest that may be charged on a credit transaction, such as a promissory note, that requires the payment of interest. Usury laws vary from state to state.

Venture capitalist. Venture capitalists look to invest in new and expanding companies based on their future prospects. They usually seek to earn between five to ten times their initial investment within a certain time frame. Their primary goal is rapid capital appreciation.

Wet garbage. This term is defined as anything organic, such as food scraps, vegetable trimmings, landscaping debris, or even pet waste. This also includes paper products and other nontoxic, biodegradable items.

Notes

_____
_____
_____
_____
_____
_____
_____
_____
_____
_____
_____
_____
_____
_____
_____
_____
_____
_____
_____
_____
_____
_____
_____
_____
_____
_____
_____
_____

Appendix B

Small Business Development Center
State Directors' Offices

Small Business Development Centers (SBDCs) can be excellent sources of assistance and information. Besides being a helpful reference resource, SBDCs provide start-up information and sponsor business-oriented seminars. These centers, which are usually located on college and university campuses, are available in every state. To find the SBDC nearest you, contact your state's SBDC headquarters that is featured in this appendix. They will be able to refer you to the SBDC nearest you.

If you have a personal computer with a modem, you can find a list of your state's SBDCs by calling the U.S. Small Business Administration's electronic bulletin board system (BBS). The BBS provides a variety of other business-related information as well. This service is provided free and can be very handy and useful for the beginning business game player. Telecommunications settings are eight data bits, one stop bit, no parity. To log on to the system, dial:

SBA Online
(800) 697-4636 (limited access)
(900) 463-4636 (full access)
(202) 401-9600 (D.C. Metro Area)

Another electronic bulletin board you can access that features a database for SBDCs is the Small Business Advancement Electronic Resource. For more information on this additional business resource, call:

Small Business Advancement Electronic Resource
(501) 450-5377

Alabama

Alabama SBDC Consortium
University of Alabama at Birmingham
Medical Towers Building
1717 11th Avenue South, Suite 419
Birmingham, AL 35294-4410
(205) 934-7260
FAX (205) 934-7645

Alaska

Alaska SBDC
University of Alaska – Anchorage
430 West Seventh Avenue, Suite 110
Anchorage, AK 99501
(907) 274-7232
FAX (907) 274-9524

Arizona

Arizona SBDC Network
2411 West 14th Street, Suite 132
Tempe, AZ 85281
(602) 731-8720
FAX (602) 731-8729

Arkansas

Arkansas SBDC
University of Arkansas at Little Rock
100 South Main, Suite 401
Little Rock, AR 72201
(501) 324-9043
FAX (501) 324-9049

California

California SBDC Program
Department of Commerce
801 K Street, Suite 1700
Sacramento, CA 95814
(916) 324-5068
FAX (916) 322-5084

Colorado

Colorado SBDC
Colorado Office of Business Development
1625 Broadway, Suite 1710
Denver, CO 80202
(303) 892-3840
FAX (303) 892-3848

Connecticut

Connecticut SBDC
University of Connecticut
2 Bourn Place, U-94
Storrs, CT 06269-5094
(860) 486-4518
FAX (860) 486-1576

Delaware

Delaware SBDC
University of Delaware
102 MBNA
America Hall
Newark, DE 19716
(302) 831-2747
FAX (302) 831-1423

District of Columbia

District of Columbia SBDC
Howard University
2600 Sixth Street NW, Room 125
Washington, DC 20059
(202) 806-1550
FAX (202) 806-1777

Florida

Florida SBDC Network
University of West Florida
Downtown Center
19 West Garden Street, Suite 300
Pensacola, FL 32501
(904) 444-2060
FAX (904) 444-2070

Georgia

Georgia SBDC
University of Georgia
Chicopee Complex
1180 East Broad Street
Athens, GA 30602-5412
(706) 542-6762
FAX (706) 542-6776

Hawaii

Hawaii SBDC Network
University of Hawaii at Hilo
200 West Kawili Street
Hilo, HI 96720-4091
(808) 933-7513
FAX (808) 933-7683

Idaho

Idaho SBDC
Boise State University
1910 University Drive
Boise, ID 83725
(208) 426-1640
FAX (208) 426-3877

Illinois

Illinois SBDC
Department of Commerce and
** Community Affairs**
620 East Adams Street, 6th Floor
Springfield, IL 62701
(217) 524-5856
FAX (217) 524-0171

Indiana

Indiana SBDC
Economic Development Council
One North Capitol, Suite 420
Indianapolis, IN 46204
(317) 264-6871
FAX (317) 264-3102

Iowa

Iowa SBDC
Iowa State University
137 Lynn Avenue
Ames, IA 50014-7126
(515) 292-6351
FAX (515) 292-0020

Kansas

Kansas SBDC
State Office
214 Southwest 6th Street, Suite 105
Topeka, KS 66603
(785) 296-6514
FAX (785) 291-3261

Kentucky

Kentucky SBDC
University of Kentucky
Center for Entrepreneurship
225 Business and Economics Building
Lexington, KY 40506-0034
(606) 257-7668
FAX (606) 323-1907

Louisiana

Louisiana SBDC
College of Business Administration 2-57
Northeast Louisiana University
700 University Avenue
Monroe, LA 71209-6435
(318) 342-5506
FAX (318) 342-5510

Maine

Maine SBDC
University of Southern Maine
96 Falmouth Street
P.O. Box 9300
Portland, ME 04103-9300
(207) 780-4420
FAX (207) 780-4810

Maryland

Maryland SBDC
University of Maryland
7100 Baltimore Avenue, Suite 401
College Park, MD 21204
(301) 403-8300
FAX (301) 403-8303

Massachusetts

Massachusetts SBDC
University of Massachusetts – Amherst
School of Management, Room 205
Amherst, MA 01003
(413) 545-6301
FAX (413) 545-1273

Michigan

Michigan SBDC State Office
2727 Second Avenue, Suite 107
Detroit, MI 48201
(313) 964-1798
FAX (313) 964-3648

Minnesota

Minnesota SBDC
Minnesota Department of Economic
** Development**
500 Metro Square
121 7th Place East
St. Paul, MN 55101-2146
(651) 297-1301
FAX (651) 296-1290

Mississippi

Mississippi SBDC
University of Mississippi
Old Chemistry Building, Suite 216
University, MS 38677
(601) 232-5001
FAX (601) 232-5650

Missouri

Missouri SBDC
University of Missouri
300 University Place
Columbia, MO 65211
(573) 882-0344
FAX (573) 884-4297

Montana

Montana SBDC
Montana Department of Commerce
1424 Ninth Avenue
Helena, MT 59620
(406) 444-4780
FAX (406) 444-2808

Nebraska

Nebraska Business Development Center
University of Nebraska at Omaha
1313 Farnam on the mall, Suite 132
Omaha, NE 68182
(402) 554-2521
FAX (402) 554-3747

Nevada

Nevada SBDC
University of Nevada – Reno
College of Business Administration – 032
1664 North Virginia Street
Reno, NV 89557-0100
(702) 784-1717
FAX (702) 784-4337

New Hampshire

New Hampshire SBDC
University of New Hampshire
108 McConnell Hall
Durham, NH 03824
(603) 862-2200
FAX (603) 862-4876

New Jersey

New Jersey SBDC
Rutgers University
180 University Avenue
Newark, NJ 07102
(201) 648-5950
FAX (201) 648-1110

New Mexico

New Mexico SBDC
Santa Fe Community College
P.O. Box 4187
Santa Fe, NM 87502-4187
(505) 438-1362
FAX (505) 438-1237

New York

New York State SBDC
State University of New York
State U Plaza, S-527
Albany, NY 12246
(518) 443-5398
FAX (518) 465-4992

North Carolina

North Carolina SBDC
University of North Carolina
333 Fayettville Street Mall, Suite 150
Raleigh, NC 27601-1742
(919) 715-7272
FAX (919) 715-7777

North Dakota

North Dakota SBDC
University of North Dakota
118 Gamble Hall, UND, Box 7308
Grand Forks, ND 58202
(701) 777-3700
FAX (701) 777-3225

Ohio

Ohio SBDC
77 South High Street, 28th Floor
P.O. Box 1001
Columbus, OH 43266-0101
(614) 466-2711
FAX (614) 466-0829

Oklahoma

Oklahoma SBDC
Southeastern Oklahoma State University
517 University
Durant, OK 74701
(405) 924-0277
FAX (405) 920-7471
(800) 522-6154

Oregon

Oregon SBDC
Lane Community College
44 West Broadway, Suite 501
Eugene, OR 97401-3201
(541) 726-2250
FAX (541) 345-6006

Pennsylvania

Pennsylvania SBDC
University of Pennsylvania
The Wharton School
444 Vance Hall, 3733 Spruce Street
Philadelphia, PA 19104-6374
(215) 898-1219
FAX (215) 573-2135

Rhode Island

Rhode Island SBDC
Bryant College
1150 Douglas Pike
Smithfield, RI 02917
(401) 232-6111
FAX (401) 232-6933

South Carolina

The Frank L. Roddey SBDC
University of South Carolina
College of Business Administration
Columbia, SC 29208
(803) 777-4907
FAX (803) 777-4403

South Dakota

South Dakota SBDC
University of South Dakota
414 East Clark Street
Vermillion, SD 57069
(605) 677-5279
FAX (605) 677-5273

Tennessee

Tennessee SBDC
University of Memphis
South Campus, Building 1, Room 101
Campus Box 526324
Memphis, TN 38152-6324
(901) 678-2500
FAX (901) 678-4072

Texas – Regional Offices

North Texas – Dallas SBDC
Bill J. Priest Institute for Economic Development
1402 Corinth Street
Dallas, TX 75215
(214) 860-5835
FAX (214) 860-5813

University of Houston SBDC
University of Houston
1100 Louisiana, Suite 500
Houston, TX 77002
(713) 752-8444
FAX (713) 756-1500

Northwest Texas SBDC
Texas Tech University
2579 South Loop 289, Suite 114
Lubbock, TX 79423
(806) 745-3973
FAX (806) 745-1637

UTSA South Texas Border SBDC
UTSA Downtown Center
1222 North Main Street, Suite 450
San Antonio, TX 78212
(210) 458-2450
FAX (210) 458-2464

Utah

Utah SBDC
Salt Lake Community College
1623 South State Street
Salt Lake City, UT 84115
(801) 957-3480
FAX (801) 957-3489

Vermont

Vermont SBDC
Vermont Technical College
P.O. Box 422
Randolph, VT 05060
(802) 728-9101
FAX (802) 728-3026

Virginia

Virginia SBDC
901 East Byrd Street, Suite 1800
Richmond, VA 23219
(804) 371-8253
FAX (804) 225-3384

Washington

Washington SBDC
Washington State University
501 Johnson Tower
P.O. Box 644851
Pullman, WA 99164-4851
(509) 335-1576
FAX (509) 335-0949

West Virginia

West Virginia SBDC
950 Kanawha Boulevard, East
Charleston, WV 25301
(304) 558-2960
FAX (304) 558-0127

Wisconsin

Wisconsin SBDC
University of Wisconsin Extension
432 North Lake Street, Room 423
Madison, WI 53706
(608) 263-7794
FAX (608) 263-7830

Wyoming

WSBDC/State Network Office
P.O. Box 3922
Laramie, WY 82071-3922
(307) 766-3505
FAX (307) 766-3406

Appendix C

National and State Business Publications

One of the most vital aspects of operating a successful business is staying well informed on both national and state-specific trends and stories in areas such as business, industry, and technology. In addition, you'll also want to stay abreast of upcoming legislation that may change how you do business or that may cost you more money in new taxes or labor requirements. By being on the cutting edge of new information, you can beat your competition in seizing a new market niche, securing the latest technological equipment, or grabbing a larger part of your target market. In short, your efforts of staying informed on national and local business-oriented news may mean increased sales or new opportunities for your business.

Reading national and state business publications is one of the best ways to stay informed. National newspapers, such as *The Wall Street Journal*, and local newspapers are excellent sources. To familiarize you with some of the nation's prominent business magazines, and magazines specific to a particular state, this appendix features two listings of business magazines, respectively.

Review the listings at your convenience and consider subscribing to one or more of the publications. The phone numbers provided for each magazine will enable you to inquire about subscription information or to request more details about the publication's editorial content and special features.

National Business Publications

ASBA Today
American Small Business Association
(800) 942-2722

Bi-monthly publication edited for the ASBA and its members. Features articles on business, money, benefits, health, and grass roots information.

The Business Owner
(800) 634-0605

A monthly magazine aimed at the small biz owner. Covers a variety of biz topics and issues.

Business Start-Ups
Entrepreneur, Inc.
(714) 261-2325

Monthly publication that contains information on starting and running a business. Special emphasis on franchising and related business opportunities.

BusinessWeek
(212) 512-2641

A weekly magazine that features general business news, new products, and articles on a number of timely issues and topics affecting our nation's business, economy, and society.

Entrepreneur
Entrepreneur, Inc.
(800) 274-6229

Monthly publication that features information on running a small business.

Fast Company
(800) 688-1545

A biz magazine for companies that think creatively, move fast, try new ideas, and are looking at tomorrow today.

Home Office Computing
Scholastic, Inc.
(212) 505-4220

Monthly publication edited for the home-based biz owner with news and information on getting the most from equipment.

IB: Independent Business
Group IV Communications, Inc.
(805) 496-6156

Bi-monthly publication of the NFIB with focus on practical advice for the operation of a small business. Also includes articles on governmental affairs affecting small business.

In Business
J.G. Press, Inc.
(610) 967-4135

Bi-monthly publication edited for entrepreneurs. Articles focus on financing, tax planning, cashflow management, staffing, and marketing.

Inc.
(800) 234-0999

Inc. provides managers of small to mid-sized privately held companies with monthly information on management approaches in finance, marketing, and personnel, as well as profiles of leading growth companies and analyses of economic and policy trends affecting the contemporary small growth firm.

Industry Week Growing Companies
(216) 931-9264

Monthly publication addressing the unique concerns of manufacturing leaders and their companies.

Nation's Business
U.S. Chamber of Commerce
(202) 463-5690

A publication of the U.S. Chamber of Commerce, *Nation's Business*, is a helpful source of emerging trends and issues facing small business.

Sales and Marketing Management
Bill Communications, Inc.
(212) 592-6300

A monthly magazine that provides helpful information on sales and marketing issues and trends that help business succeed.

Small Business Opportunities
Harris Publications, Inc.
(212) 807-7100

A monthly magazine that offers practical advice to entrepreneurs, plus regular features on numerous franchise opportunities throughout the country.

Spare Time
Kipen Publishing Corporation
(414) 543-8110

For anyone interested in money-making opportunities, selling (full- or spare-time), starting a business, franchise openings, and profitable sidelines. Articles deal with home training programs, successful selling tips, and emphasizes individual success stories.

Success Magazine
(800) 234-7324

A monthly magazine for the entrepreneurial mind.

Your Company
Time Warner, Inc.
(212) 522-1212

Quarterly publication sent at no charge to corporate cardmembers as a benefit of membership. Provides vital, concise, practical, and timely advice to small biz owners seeking to better manage their companies.

Working at Home
(800) 352-8202

A quarterly magazine for you home body entrepreneurs.

State Business Publications

Alabama

Business Alabama Monthly
(334) 473-6269

Alaska

Alaska Business Monthly
(907) 276-4373

Arizona

Arizona Business Gazette
(602) 271-7300
www.azresource.com

Arizona Business Magazine
(602) 277-6045

The Arizona Daily Star
(520) 753-4176
(520) 753-4107

The Arizona Republic
(602) 444-8000

The Business Journal
(602) 230-8400

Today's Arizona Woman Magazine
(602) 945-5000

Tribune Newspapers
(602) 898-6500
www.tribaz.com

Arkansas

the Arkansas Advantage
Arkansas Industrial Development Commission
(501) 682-1121

Arkansas Business
(501) 372-1443

Taking Care of Business
(501) 682-1121

California

Los Angeles Business Journal
(213) 549-5225

Orange County Business Journal
(714) 833-8373

Sacramento Business Journal
(916) 447-7661

State Business Publications (continued)

California (continued)

San Diego Business Journal
(619) 277-6359

San Francisco Business Times
(415) 989-2522

Santa Clara Valley Business Journal
(408) 295-3800

Colorado

CBM: Colorado Business Magazine
(303) 397-7600

The Denver Business Journal
(303) 837-3500

Connecticut

Business Times
(203) 782-1420

CBIA News
(860) 244-1900

Greater Danbury Business Digest
(203) 798-7063

Hartford Business Journal
(860) 236-9998

Delaware

There are no state-specific publications for
Delaware.

District of Columbia

Business & Health Magazine
(202) 547-0855

Washington Business Journal
(703) 875-2200

Florida

Broward/Palm Beach/Miami Review
(305) 377-3721

Business in Broward
(305) 563-8805

Daily Business Review
(305) 377-3721

Florida Trend
(813) 821-5800

Gainsville/Ocala Business
(850) 622-2995

Jacksonville Business Journal
(850) 396-3502

Miami Business Magazine
(305) 379-1118

Orlando Business Journal
(407) 649-8470

South Florida Business Journal
(954) 359-2100

Georgia

American City Business Journal
(404) 249-1000

Area Development Magazine
Halcyon Business Publications, Inc.
(516) 338-0900
(800) 735-2732
www.area-development.com

Atlanta Business Chronicle
(404) 249-1000

Atlanta Business Journal
(770) 969-7711

The Atlanta Small Business Monthly, Inc.
(770) 446-5434

Georgia Trend
(770) 931-9410

Hawaii

Hawaii Business
(808) 537-9500

Hawaii Business League
(808) 533-6819

Island Business Magazine
(808) 524-7400

NFIB Hawaii
(808) 422-2163

Pacific Business News
(808) 596-2021

Today's Honolulu Business
(808) 521-8555

Idaho

The Idaho Business Review
(208) 336-3768

Idaho State Journal
(208) 232-4161

Idaho Statesman
(208) 377-6200

Illinois

Argus Business
(312) 726-7277

Business Marketing
(312) 649-5309

Chicago
(312) 222-8999

Crain's Chicago Business
(312) 649-5411

Women's Business Journal
(312) 867-7700

Indiana

Business People
(219) 426-0124

Indiana Business Magazine
(317) 692-1200

Indianapolis Business Journal
(317) 634-6200

Indianapolis C.E.O.
(317) 257-8000

Issues In Business
(317) 257-8000
(800) 264-4236

Lafayette Business Digest
(317) 742-6918

Iowa

Business and Industry Magazine
(515) 225-2545

Business Record
(515) 288-3336

Kansas

Johnson County Business Times
(913) 649-8778

Kansas City Business Journal
(816) 421-5900

Mid-America Commerce and Industry
(785) 272-5280

Kentucky

Business Bulletin
(502) 695-4700

Business First
(502) 583-1731

Louisiana

Business Report
(504) 928-1700

The Lafayette Business Journal
(318) 289-6340

Maine

There are no state-specific publications for Maine.

Maryland

Baltimore Business Journal
(410) 576-1161

The Daily Record
(410) 752-1717

The Maryland Entrepreneur
(301) 405-2144

Metropolitan Business News
(410) 433-0020

Phillips Business Information
(301) 340-1520

State Business Publications (continued)

Massachusetts

Boston Business Journal
(617) 330-1000

Business Worcester
(508) 755-8004

Creative Business
(617) 424-1368

Journal of Commerce
(617) 523-3582

New England Economic Review
(617) 973-3403

Michigan

Corporate Detroit Magazine
(313) 345-3300

Crain's Detroit Business
(313) 446-6000
www.crainsdetroit.com

Detroiter Magazine
(313) 964-4000

Grand Rapids Press
(616) 222-5411

Lansing State Journal
(517) 377-1020

Minnesota

Business Ethics Magazine
(612) 879-0695

Corporate Report – Minnesota
(612) 338-4288

Minnesota Business Opportunity
(612) 844-0400

Successful Business
(507) 285-7600

Twin Cities Business Monthly
(612) 339-7571

Mississippi

Coast Business Journal
(228) 594-0004

Jackson Business Journal
(601) 956-0756

Mississippi Business Journal
(601) 364-1000

Missouri

Columbia Business Times
(573) 499-1830

Ingram's
(816) 842-9994

Kansas City Business Journal
(816) 421-5900

Missouri Business
(573) 634-3511

Springfield Business Times
(417) 831-3238

Montana

Big Sky Business Journal
(406) 259-2309

Montana Magazine
(406) 443-2842

Nebraska

Lincoln Business Journal
(402) 434-7750

Omaha Business Journal
(402) 330-1760

Nevada

Business Beat
(702) 454-9545

Nevada Business Journal
(702) 735-7003

New Hampshire

BNH: The Business of New Hampshire
(603) 626-6354

New Hampshire Business Review
(603) 624-1442

New Jersey

Mercer Business
(609) 586-2056

New Jersey Business
New Jersey Business and Industry Association
(201) 882-5004
www.njbmagazine.com

New Mexico

Albuquerque Journal
(505) 823-3800

New Mexico Business Journal
(505) 243-3444

New Mexico Business Weekly
(505) 292-6152

New York

Brooklyn Business Journal
(718) 625-7500

Business First: Newspaper of Buffalo
(716) 882-6200

Capital District Business Review
(518) 437-9855

Central New York Business Journal
(315) 446-3510

Crain's New York Business
(212) 210-0100

Hudson Valley Business Journal
(914) 258-4007

International Business
(914) 381-7700

Long Island Business News
(516) 737-1700

Long Island Magazine
(516) 499-4400

Rochester Business Journal
(716) 546-8303

Rochester Business Magazine
(716) 458-8280

Rockland County Business Journal
(914) 258-4008

Syracuse Business
(315) 472-6911

Westchester County Business Journal
(914) 347-5200

North Carolina

American City Business Journal
(704) 375-7404

The Business Journal of Charlotte
(800) 948-5323
www.amcity.com/charlotte

Business Leader
(919) 872-7077

Business Life
(336) 854-4260

Business North Carolina
(704) 523-6987

Capital Opportunities for Small Business
SBTDC
(919) 717-7272

Carolina Business
(919) 633-5106

NC Entrepreneur
(910) 854-5711

North Carolina
(919) 828-0758

Triad Business News
(910) 854-3001
www.hpe.com/hpe/tbn

Triangle Business Journal
(919) 878-0010
www.amcity.com/triangle

Triangle East Business Journal
(252) 478-4802

State Business Publications (continued)

North Dakota

There are no state-specific publications for North Dakota.

Ohio

Business First: The Newspaper of Greater Columbus
(614) 461-4040

The Clevelander – Growth Association
(216) 621-3300

Ohio Magazine
(614) 461-5083

Small Business Journal
(513) 579-8725

Toledo Business Journal
(419) 244-8200

Oklahoma

Community Developer
(405) 815-6552

Oklahoma Business News
(405) 521-1405

Oklahoma Observer
(405) 525-5582

Oregon

Business Journal
(503) 581-7290

Oregon Business
(800) 367-3466

Portland Business Journal
(503) 274-8733

Pennsylvania

Central Penn Business Journal
(717) 236-4300

Eastern Pennsylvania Business Journal
(610) 807-9619

Northeast Pennsylvania Business Journal
(717) 283-9271

Pennsylvania Business Central
(814) 867-2222

Pennsylvania CPA Journal
(215) 735-2635

Pittsburgh Business Times
(412) 481-6397

Rhode Island

Providence Business News
(401) 273-2201

South Carolina

The Charleston Regional Business Journal
(843) 723-7702

South Carolina Business and Economic Review
The Darla Moore School of Business
(803) 777-2510

South Carolina Business Journal
(803) 799-4601

South Carolina Business Opportunities
(803) 737-0686

South Dakota

Business Page
(605) 336-2218

South Dakota Business Review
(605) 677-5287

Tennessee

The Business Journal
(423) 323-7111
www.bjournal.xtn.net

Chattanooga Business Journal
(423) 629-7500

Memphis Business Journal
(901) 523-1000

Nashville Business Journal
(615) 248-2222

Nashville Business In Review
(615) 255-9792

Texas

Austin Business Journal
(512) 494-2500

Business Horizons
(214) 749-5400

Business Press
(817) 336-8300

Dallas Business Journal
(214) 696-5959

Dallas Business Review
(972) 458-2512

Houston Business Journal
(713) 688-8811

Minority Business News
(214) 369-3200

San Antonio Business Journal
(210) 341-3202

Utah

Business Source
(801) 485-3493

Utah Business
(801) 568-0114

Vermont

Business Digest
(802) 862-4109

Champlain Business Journal
(802) 862-9100

Rutland Business Journal
(802) 775-9500

Small Cities Business Journal
(802) 775-6424

Valley Business Journal
(802) 295-8747

Vermont Business Magazine
(802) 863-8038

Virginia

*The Business Journal of Tri-Cities
Tennessee/Virginia*
(423) 323-7111

Virginia Business
(804) 649-6999

Washington

Bellingham Business Journal
(360) 647-8805

Business Journal
(360) 647-8805

Business Pulse
(360) 671-3933

Journal of Business
(509) 456-5257
www.spokanejournal.com

Kitsap Business Journal
(360) 876-7900

Marple's Business Newsletters
(206) 281-9609

Peninsula Business Journal
(360) 683-3205

Puget Sound Business Journal
(206) 583-0701
www.amcity.com/seattle

Small Business Journal
(206) 241-5854

Vancouver Business Journal
(360) 695-2442

Wenatchee Business Journal
(509) 663-6730

West Virginia

The State Journal
(304) 344-1630

State Business Publications (continued)

Wisconsin

The Business Journal of Milwaukee
(414) 278-7788

In-Business Magazine
(608) 246-3580

New Business Planning Guide or Business Resource Guide
(414) 287-4100

Wisconsin Woman
(414) 358-9290

Wyoming

There are no state-specific publications for Wyoming.

Appendix D
Small Business Web Sites

The World Wide Web has become a virtual treasure trove of information and tips for small business owners and entrepreneurs. Many web sites are dedicated to assisting and educating small business owners on a number of topics, ranging from general start-up considerations to financing and marketing.

As a soon-to-be entrepreneur, these web sites are terrific resources to consider when researching ideas, looking for assistance, and solving everyday biz problems.

The information, advice, and networking that's found on the Internet will truly be a shot in the arm when the rigors and training for the business game get tiring. The wealth of free information and seemingly endless number of biz sites will get your blood pumping and often inspire a second wind.

To give you a headstart in the biz game, we've compiled a list of business web sites that we know will help you stay the course and cross the finishing line in great shape. Check these web sites out when you can (or need to) and see where they lead you. Good luck!

General Small Business Sites

All Business Network
www.all-biz.com

A solid resource for small business with its features, directories, business news, and resource listings.

American Home Business Association
www.homebusiness.com

Dedicated to providing practical info and advice to the home-based entrepreneur.

Bureau of National Affairs (BNA)
www.bna.com

BNA publishes books on a variety of biz-related topics, such as labor relations, law, economics, taxation, environmental protection, safety, and other public policy and regulatory issues.

EntrepreNet
www.enterprise.org/enet

An online business power bar equivalent for new biz owners.

Entrepreneur Magazine
www.entrepreneurmag.com

A general small business site with features on biz news, franchise opportunities, and much more.

The Entrepreneur/Small Business Newsletter
www.masterlink.com

A slick list of info and articles on financing, marketing, accounting, insurance, and legal issues.

Entrepreneurial Edge
www.edgeonline.com

The web site for the magazine, *Entrepreneurial Edge*.

Fast Company Magazine
www.fastcompany.com

A site for the biz owner looking for news on the world of evolving business and new ways of working, competing, and living. This online magazine writes about the new economy and workplace. It gives you real tools to solve real problems.

Home Business EntrepreneURLs
www.windansea.com/hb/enturls.htm

An extensive listing of hot links for the home-based start-up.

Idea Cafe: The Small Business Channel
www.ideacafe.com

A fun approach to serious business! Get info on start-up financing, business communication, and chat with other entrepreneurs.

Inc. Magazine
www.inc.com

Watch out for the great biz moves and grooves on this online companion to the small business magazine, *Inc.*

Kauffman Center for Entrepreneurial Leadership
www.entreworld.com

Keep your finger on the pulse of small biz news and activity here.

The Mining Company
www.sbinformation.miningco.com

A guide for resources and links for the business rookie.

Mothers' Home Business Network
www.homeworkingmom.com

The first and largest national organization providing ideas, inspiration, and support for mothers who choose to work at home.

The National Association for the Self-Employed (NASE)
www.nase.org

A site dedicated to providing businesses with legislative info, services, and biz advice.

National Federation of Independent Business (NFIB)
www.nfibonline.com

Learn about this small biz organization and its lobbying efforts in Washington, D.C.

National Small Business United (NSBU)
www.nsbu.org

Keeps small biz owners in touch with legislative and regulatory issues that affect them.

The Oasis Press/PSI Research
www.psi-research.com

A showcase of all the small business books and software products available through the Leading Publisher of Small Business Information.

Quicken
www.quickenbiz.com

Packed with valuable info, tools, and personalized services — and dedicated to business success.

SBA Hotlist
www.sba.gov/hotlist

More than 1,000 small business web sites to choose from!

SBA Online
U.S. Small Business Administration (SBA)
www.sbaonline.sba.gov

A guide to all the small business programs, services, and resources available through the SBA.

Service Corps of Retired Executives (SCORE)
www.score.org

Round the clock access to small biz counseling services, workshop info, and a rich database of resources. And it's all free thru the SBA.

Small & Home-based Business Links
www.bizoffice.com

Provides links to home-based business, entrepreneurial, and government sites. A good jumping off point for any start-up.

Small Business Advancement National Center
www.sbaer.uca.edu

Offers valuable resource information for any small business owner, plus Small Business Institute (SBI) info as well. A valuable stop on the Internet.

The Small Business Advisor
www.isquare.com

Especially for entrepreneurs with a new start-up biz — lots of books, special reports, and consulting resources available for the asking.

Small Business News Online
www.sbnpub.com

Offers solutions to the daily challenges of growing a business. Topics include management, finance, marketing, technology, health care, and personnel.

SmallbizNet
www.lowe.org

Features an electronic bookshelf and a bulletin board where you can trade tips and advice with others.

Smart Business Supersite
www.smartbiz.com

It's the how-to resource for business and start-ups.

U.S. Business Advisor
www.business.gov

A one-stop center for making electronic links to all government business sites.

Your Small Office
www.smalloffice.com

A likable site with interesting tidbits of information for small businesses. Get reviews on software and hardware, current articles for small business, or visit one of their mini-sites on taxes, business travel, web construction, or small business associations.

Working Solo Online
www.workingsolo.com

A great place to stop by to ask questions and get answers regarding running a one-person operation.

Customer Service Sites

The Right Answer: The Customer Finessing Center
www.therightanswer.com

A fun and informative site on customer service tips, training, and advice. Join their customer service pro society, take a turn in the Quiz Center, and receive free email newsletters.

The Uniform Code Council, Inc.
www.uc-council.org

Its mission is to take a global leadership role in establishing and promoting multi-industry standards for product identification and related electronic communications. The goal is to enhance efficient supply chain management, thus contributing added value to the customer.

Employer Sites

Equal Employment Opportunity Commission (EEOC)
www.eeoc.gov

Learn about your responsibilities as an employer under federal laws.

Immigration and Naturalization Service (INS)
www.ins.usdoj.gov

Visit this site to find the nearest INS office and how to comply with *Form I-9* requirements.

U.S. Department of Labor
www.dol.gov

Learn about wage and safety and health laws here. Free booklets and info are available.

Environmental Business Sites

American LabelMark/Labelmaster
www.labelmaster.com

If you need help with hazardous material labeling or further info on this aspect of business, this company can help.

Environmental Protection Agency (EPA)
www.epa.gov

For assistance in complying with federal EPA requirements. Think clean.

Financing Sites

America's Business Funding Directory
www.businessfinance.com

A free service designed to help those in need of capital find it online.

America's Small Business Financial Center
www.netearnings.com

The one-stop shop for small business insurance, loans, credit cards, and payroll services, quotes, and online applications.

American Bankers Association
www.aba.com

A good place to go for information on financial publications, sources, and advice.

Ernst & Young Entrepreneurs Services
www.ey.com

A great source for tips on financing, operating strategies, acquisitions, and expansion.

Internal Revenue Service (IRS)
www.irs.ustreas.gov

Bookmark this site. It's where to register for federal employment taxes, learn about free tax publications, and get the latest tax news.

Money Online
www.money.com

Based on *Money* magazine, this site features a list of financial sites for new start-ups.

National Association of Small Business Institute Companies (SBICs)
www.nasbic.org

Central contact agency to find the SBIC nearest you and what these offices can do for your new biz.

National Venture Capital Association (NVCA)
www.nvca.org

Designed to help you find sources of venture capital.

Quicken
www.cashfinder.com

Save yourself time and hassle and use Quicken's Business Cashfinder to get funding. This free service lets you shop online for biz loans, credit cards, lines of credit, and leases.

Venture Associates
www.Venturea.com

A Denver financial consulting firm that offers information on finding angels, venture capital, investment bankers, management consultants, and more.

Venture Capital Online
www.vcapital.com

Information and networking opportunities for entrepreneurs and venture capitalists.

Venture-Preneurs Network
www.venturepreneurs.com

Offers services to start-ups, including locating venture capital.

Wall Street Journal Interactive Edition
www.wsj.com

An electronic version of the newspaper that features financial news, stock quotes, and biz-related articles.

Franchising Sites

Business International Sales and Opportunity Network (BISON)
www.bison1.com

The complete franchise resource with sections discussing franchise information, business loans, and franchise development. This is a site for "those serious about franchising."

Federal Trade Commission (FTC)
www.ftc.gov

Find out federal disclosure information on franchise opportunities here and much more.

Franchise Times
www.franchisetimes.com

A magazine for those seeking various franchise opportunities and how to get the most for their money.

FranInfo
www.neosoft.com/~frannet/

A site dedicated to giving you the most complete how-to advice and tips on the world of franchising.

International Franchise Association (IFA)
www.franchise.org

Check out all the great resources they feature on their site, from which franchise is right for you to getting legal information.

Marketing Sites

American Business Information (ABI)
www.abii.com

ABI's site provides access to numerous databases, including the Yellow Pages online and other resources. There's a fee for some services and a required membership.

American Marketing Association (AMA)
www.ama.com

Promotes education and professional development in marketing.

Connecting Online
www.connectingonline.com

Tidbits on public relations and using the Internet for marketing your biz.

Guerrilla Marketing Online
www.gmarketing.com

Offers a weekly column on marketing strategies, as well as write-ups on other helpful sites for the guerrilla entrepreneur.

The Internet Marketing Center
www.marketingtips.com

Show how to start and promote virtually any business, product, or service on the Internet.

Newsletter Resources
www.newsletterinfo.com

Plenty of free advice from an expert on how to get the most marketing home runs from a newsletter.

U.S. Census Bureau
www.census.gov

Your online source for social, demographic, and economic information and data.

U.S. Patent and Trademark Office
www.uspto.gov

If you'll want to register a trademark, service mark, or trade name for your new start-up, then visit this site for the low-down on how to get the job done.

Index

Don't Let Your Quest to Start Your Business Stop Yet!

After all, your success is our success...

1 At PSI Research and The Oasis Press,° we take pride in helping you and two million other businesses grow. We hope that *Start Your Business* has helped you move toward a successful business start-up, but we also want you to know that we'll be here for you after you open your doors for business too.

On the following pages, we offer a brief sampling of *The Successful Business Library* — books and software that will help you solve your day-to-day issues and prepare you for unexpected problems your business may face down the road. We offer up-to-date and practical business solutions, which are easy to use and understand. Call for a complete catalog or let our knowledgeable sales representatives point you in the right direction.

Committed to keeping you up-to-date...

2 Occasionally our fast-paced world doesn't allow us to get you the most current information in print until after you have already made an investment in one of our products. To solve this problem, we have created a resource on the Internet that can react to immediate changes in laws, regulations, and other business factors that could affect your business in the future. Our comprehensive Web site, *www.psi-research.com*, is designed to help you find the information you need. Just look for the link for *Start Your Business* or our Business Solutions for the most current contacts and updates.

visit us at http://www.psi-research.com

Your input means a lot to us...

3 Our doors are always open — whether it's to find out about a product that can assist you in building a smart, well-prepared business; to tell us about your business' own success story; or, to suggest ways we could improve our products for you — and we look forward to your call. For more information about our products or to request a complete catalog, call 1-800-228-2275 between 6:30 AM to 4:00 PM, Pacific Time. Our Web site also features a 24-hour online store to order any of our products, as well as a forms for comments and catalog requests.

Let *SmartStart* pave your way through today's complex business environment.

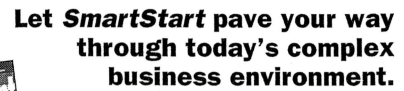

You may be like more than 35 million other Americans – you dream of owning a business. In fact, there has never been a better time to start a small business. According to a recent research study by the Entrepreneurial Research Consortium, one out of three U.S. households has someone who is involved in a small business startup. With statistics like these, the odds seem to be in your favor... until you start dealing with the many regulations, laws, and financial requirements placed on 21st century business owners.

SmartStart Your (State*) Business goes a step beyond other business how-to books and provides you with:

X Each book is state specific, with information and resources that are unique. This gives you an advantage over other general business start-up books that have no way of providing current local information you will need;

X Quick reference to the most current mailing and Internet addresses and telephone numbers for the federal, state, local, and private agencies that will help get your business up and running;

X State population statistics, income and consumption rates, major industry trends, and overall business incentives to give you a better picture of doing business in your state; and

X Logical checklists, sample forms, and a complete sample business plan to assist you with the numerous start-up details.

SmartStart is your roadmap to avoid legal and financial pitfalls and direct you through the bureaucratic red tape that often entangles fledgling entrepreneurs. This is your all-in-one resource tool that will give you a jump start on planning for your business.

SmartStart Your (State*) Business
$19.95, paperback

* When ordering, be sure to tell us which state you are interested in receiving.

Order direct from The Oasis Press®

You can order any Successful Business Library title directly from The Oasis Press.® We would be happy to hear from you and assist you in finding the right titles for your small business needs at:

1-800-228-2275

Because *SmartStart* is a new state-specific series, new states are being released every month, please call to confirm a state's scheduled release date — or check with your favorite bookstore.

Moonlighting: Earn a Second Income at Home
Paperback: $15.95

Pages: 240

ISBN: 1-55571-406-4

It is projected that half of the homes in America are expected to house some type of business in the next few years. *Moonlighting* takes the idea of starting your own home-based business a step further. It will show you, in realistic and achievable steps, how you can initially pursue a business dream part-time, instead of quitting your job and being without a financial safety net. This confidence building guide will help motivate you by showing you the best steps toward setting your plan in motion.

Home Business Made Easy
Paperback: $19.95

Pages: 233

ISBN: 1-55571-428-5

An easy-to-follow guide to help you decide if starting a home-based business is right for you. Takes you on a tour of 153 home business options to start your decision process. Author David Hanania also advises potential business owners on the fiscal aspects of small startups, from financing sources to dealing with the IRS.

Which Business?
Paperback: $18.95

Pages: 376

ISBN: 1-55571-342-4

A compendium of real business opportunities, not just "hot" new ventures that often have limited earning potential. *Which Business?* will help you define your skills and interests by exploring your dreams and how you think about business. Learn from profiles of 24 business areas, reviewing how each got their start and problems and successes that they have experienced.

Friendship Marketing
Paperback: $18.95

Pages: 187

ISBN: 1-55571-399-8

If you have every wondered how to combine business success and personal signficance, author Gerald Baron has numerous practical suggestions. After years of working with executives and entrepreneurs, he's found that business success and personal meaning can share common ground. Using dozens of examples, he shows how building relationships is the key to business development and personal fulfillment.

CALL TO PLACE AN ORDER
— or —
TO RECEIVE A FREE CATALOG

1-800-228-2275

International Orders (541) 479-9464   Fax Orders (541) 476-1479
Web site http://www.psi-research.com   Email sales@psi-research.com

PSI Research P.O. Box 3727 Central Point, Oregon 97502 U.S.A.